About the Author

Graham and Karen Badrock live in Bright Victoria, just voted the 'best town in Victoria'. Along with that recognition comes a myriad of complex and interesting problems that need to be dealt with daily. Covid19 certainly threw a spanner in the works. Prior to the restrictions, they were able to escape to the South Pacific, travelling on a cruise, then straight back into one of the world's harshest lock downs. The need to resort to building model ships, playing golf wearing a mask, and then even managing to achieve the golfer's ultimate, two holes in one on the same hole three weeks apart, but with no one to celebrate with. He has always told his children, now adults, that 'sometimes it's hard being a parent, but just go with the flow', and that included five hours fishing with no result. Sometimes you win, and sometimes second, but never last.

The Quest for the
Last Coconut

Graham Badrock

The Quest for the
Last Coconut

Vanguard Press

DEDICATION

To, Banjo, Mya, Ivy, Ella and Harriet.

Chapter 1

We have been travelling for several weeks and have finally come to a standstill. No, we are still talking, my wife and I, but we had earlier decided to stay in one location for some time. Our location is Discovery Park, Fraser Street in Hervey Bay. Packed in like sardines ready for sale. Our neighbours in this little part of Queensland are a different dynamic than we have come across in our past travels.

The male of the species is a complex character, let alone stick him in a caravan park at close quarters with others. I have gradually been thinking, 'is this what my life will be like in ten to fifteen years?' Older, well that goes without saying, but will I be polishing my tow ball like the elderly caravanner along the line? A smallish man, maybe in his early seventies, bald head, long shorts, and a natty little white moustache. 'Boating' shoes, no socks, and a crisp white shirt. His wife, small and hardly seen at all. Their caravan of choice is a large 20' Royal Flair. Gleaming in the sun, its silver sides as new as the day it was purchased. No dust and certainly no dirt would even have the cheek to adhere on its shiny surface. The matching vehicle was a brand spanking new, white Land Rover Discovery. One night the area was fortunate to be blessed with a few showers of rain. There he was first thing in the morning, out wiping down the offending water and to my amazement polishing his chrome tow ball.

As we walk around our little world and see the comings and goings it's like the clans of Scotland. Each evening, around four thirty p.m. give or take a minute, little groups can be seen huddled under awnings discussing the day's activities. 'Happy hour,' as it's known, is one of those secret rituals that occur in most caravan parks we have visited. 'They', those who have been invited to join in, do appear to be quietly proud of their invite and can be seen ever so slightly staring at the 'others' who have not been included. We have occasionally been in one of these clan meetings and the conversation goes something like this.

"Oh, so what's the go with your new reversing system, and what's cooking on the new Weber barby tonight?" All topics that would bore people who stay in hotels and resorts to death. Not relevant and of no interest to anyone apart from the clans.

The standard of your caravan, size, length, tow ball weight and such can be a determining factor in deciding which group you belong to. Older and smaller size vans are on the outer as are people in tents. People in motor homes have been known not to receive the all-important nod and a wave as they pass while driving out on the open roads. One of our dear friends, who has since gone to the big caravan park in the sky, Frank Heydon, stated often, "no, we don't wave as they don't count in the caravan world, just interlopers." Frank and his wife, Iris, were one of the old timers caravanners, small van, no toilet or shower, but they travelled all over Australia throughout their many years dragging the van.

Speaking of modern facilities in caravans today, most of those who are of a certain age, retired and escaping their families like us, do appreciate having a toilet and shower inside the van. With the need to answer the call of nature more frequently, no one finds the need to wander out at night to the nearest amenity block. Cane toads, snakes and lizards are always a consideration especially if you cannot find your way or your glasses in times of need. One of the things on the other side of the equation is the ability to become deaf at the drop of a hat. Lying in bed, no more than five metres away from the little toilet hidden behind the vinyl folding door, the noises are a bit close to home. Shut your eyes and think of England then pretend to go to sleep. That usually does the trick.

Our neighbours now are a couple in their mid-seventies I would think. He tall and distinguished and sporting a good head of white hair. While his poor long-suffering wife tends to his every need. "Rob, would you like me to do your ironing now?" If my wife asked me such a thing, I would think she really has something to hide. We have managed to bring clothing with us for our eight weeks away that is wrinkle-free and doesn't need to go anywhere near an ironing board. They are both dressed in lovely colours, bright and crisp, and sparkling white sneakers and matching white socks. His neatly pulled halfway up his shins, while she, those nice white fluffy things.

I was taking our dog, Stan, for his morning walk at seven a.m. and Rob was already dressed in his bright pink shirt, long and neatly ironed denim shorts, nice belt and combed coiffured head. He was delicately hanging out his washing next to the laundry block. Considering the wash cycle is a little under forty minutes, it must have been an incredibly early start. His wife sauntered out around eight a.m. still in her dressing gown. I think I know who is trusted with the washing in their house.

On our site, we have erected privacy screens to the sides and on the end facing the road. Not to be unsocial just to stop bloody Stan from running out and annoying the world. While they, Rob and his wife, have produced the cleanest and pristine site known to man. As you gaze in on their little kingdom, the visitor will notice two flags flying proudly above their caravan. Both are AFL teams, one Hawthorn and the other Western Bulldogs. I think this is some form of undercover, "come and talk to me, I'm from Victoria" ploy. And I must admit this seems to work wonders. People will often be seen stopping for a chat about this and that. "Oh, you follow such and such," then say trying to strike up one of those fleeting friendships that are part of being one of Australia's Grey Nomads. We have come across this many times on our travels, a bit like, "here we are, come and ask us about our life."

Anyhow back to Bob and his wife. From what we have seen, it would always be Rob and never Bob. Rob, as we speak, has been diligently packing things away for their departure in the morning. I don't know if we are one out of the box, but when we leave a site, the longest it will take is around forty-five minutes at the most to pack everything away and hitch up and drive off. Rob has been at it for hours, toiling so hard that he is now asleep. His dutiful wife sitting at his feet, well not really, just on the chair beside her knight in a pink shirt, white shorts, neatly ironed and those fashionable long white socks and runners. A picture of contentment. I have noticed two sides to our Rob. They seemed to be all over each other and appeared to have the desire to pass the time together, but we also heard those odd words one morning. He, "if you're not nice to me I will be not happy and may be really grumpy to you," said in a tone that did not reflect the same attitude that came across with his new best friends. Not us but the other couple immediately behind his site.

I should mention that as we are in this caravan park for over three weeks, it is fascinating to see all the comings and goings every day. Our neighbours out the front, if you recall, he was the one who let his dog terrorise poor Stan in our van, have left to terrorise others and we now have a couple around the same age as us. They arrived yesterday towing their little old pop-top caravan. He was tinkering around setting up while his partner was nowhere to be seen. We think she tottered off into her en-suite and was not noticed for some time. He, in stock standard attire, dark blue polo shirt, tucked into denim shorts sauntered over to thank us for the folding table that we were trying to give away.

Then out she came. Coffee cup in hand, wearing a long blue chiffon-style dress, sparkling white blouse, and carefully coiffured blond hair. To finish off the overall effect of a stunned mullet, she was elevated on a pair of glistening gold shoes. A look of bewilderment was etched on her face. It was like, "where are we, and why am I in front of this old and tiny pop-top caravan thingy?" We smiled as we got in our car, hoping for a reaction, but there was nothing. I was beginning to think we were invisible. He was still busy now doing something important, but I really haven't got a clue what it is. Oh well, everyone to their own, but we still haven't seen his partner again. It must be quite difficult secreting yourself away from the world.

We were blessed, well not really, but it does sound nice and warm and fuzzy when you say it quickly with our new arrivals right behind our site. A large Jayco Expanda reversed in a couple of days ago. A young family had obviously hired the van for a few days and chose the caravan park where we are staying. Husband and wife, their three children and two small and yappy bloody dogs. He appeared to be one of those males who could and would do everything. I immediately noticed that everything had a specific place. Five seats were aligned, and five matching plastic storage boxes also in a line. Children's scooters were placed nicely according to their ascending size. Washing was hung up according to colour and size. This immediately becomes as interesting to others as it did to us. The dogs were left inside their caravan and barked at everything that flew and walked by when they were out. The parents appeared to please themselves and left their children to roam around the playground and park on their own.

The children's mother was tall and seemed to be in rather good shape, while her husband was seen wandering around his van in his underwear following his more than adequate stomach. I drew my wife's attention to their packing-up routine. She took the children off to the playground while he began the tortuous task of restacking all their possessions. One painstaking item at a time. When the opportunity came to collect the three scooters and simply toss them in the van as I would have done, he painfully picked up each one, examined it for size and colour, selected the correct one and walked back to place it in its specific location. I felt like yelling, "for god's sake, pick them all up at the same time and toss them in, you dick head!" No, of course, I didn't, but I did quietly say the same thing to our dog, Stan. I think he did understand.

New arrivals, and let's face it, we all are those sometimes. We had just been down the end of the road for our daily bit of torture. Walking for over an hour with Stan along the beach. Although this was our third time, we both agreed that somehow our walk has been extended. More about all this later. Back to the newbies, as they are called. A small new van had appeared as if by magic while we were out chasing the end of the beach. Happy, clean, and neat, that was the couple as was their setup. Annex neatly pegged, concrete pad swept and tidy. There they were sitting arms crossed and watching the world go by. Secretly I think waiting to be invited to one of the clans' get-togethers. We smiled and left them to it.

After wondering why all these people in caravans, and that does include us of course, find the need to travel all over Australia and stay in a caravan park of their choice. Is it the need to feel safe and secure among others? While I am writing this, within the space of fifteen metres we are surrounded by seven other caravans and their owners. One thing about all this is that you can literally follow the lives of others. Sound seems to carry an awful lot, and I know for one, if we lived this close to others at home, we would go away in an instant.

Enough of this, let's have a look around the area. Each morning I use the excuse of having to take Stan out for his morning constitutional. A poop and a pee or three and that's just for him. We make our way along the stretch of vans and motor homes on our right. Turn left at the laundry where he has marked his spot. A quick squat and he is done. Out through the electric gates and into Fraser Street.

On our first morning, I made the mistake of crossing the road in front of the caravan park. Directly over the road is one of those houses constructed in the 1980s. Brick and located on a large double block of land. The owner then thought it would be a great idea to build a fortress. High secure steel front fence and the house itself has the strangest of features. We have noticed that most houses in Queensland have steel security mesh on just about everything that opens or closes. Windows, doors and even tiny toilet windows on the third floor of buildings are all highly secured.

The brick fortress over the road, of course, has steel security screens all over the house but their screens are on the inside of the windows. There is obviously someone in residence who enjoys a bit of gardening as the right-hand side of their double block is completely planted with a generous crop of mature palm trees. Gilligan from Gilligan's Island would have felt very much at home on the property in Fraser Street, Hervey Bay. One thing that did spoil the illusion of their little bit of tropical heaven was the truly ferocious dog that was lurking behind the fence. As Stan and I were casually minding our own business, the bloody dog tried its best to eat its way through the steel posts separating both Stan and I from certain death. We both got such a fright that we jumped back at the same time while our would-be attacker followed our every move.

Reaching the relative safety of the end of their property we both seemed to take a breath of relief. A quick cross of the road and we were only one more street from the beach and the foreshore. Immediately to our left was one of those old Queenslander homes that was suffering a big dose of neglect. Set up on posts and quite close to the front of the property. In a complete state of decay, I was incredibly surprised that anyone would actually be living there. An old blue sedan was parked down the side of the house, so it appeared that someone was in residence. The front door was hidden behind a rusted old wrought-iron bit of framework, and to finish off the overall effect, torn and tattered curtains fluttered in the morning breeze. The front fence had seen better days, a low timber structure topped off with a few bare strands of loosely-fitted wire.

Suddenly, two ferocious dogs with a background dubious even to their parents tore out from under the house. I thought, "my god, we're going to be attacked once again and all within fifty metres." Instantly, a male of questionable background roared as his dogs tried in vain to force their way through the fence. "Come here, you bastards." They ignored him as we backed off and onto the road. The next morning, he was sitting on his front porch, wearing a dirty tracksuit pants and a torn tee shirt. No "good morning and sorry about the other day" only a glare in our direction and then back to his coffee.

When our heart rates slowed, we finally made our way to the shopping strip and over the crossing to the relative safety of the beach. 'No dogs on beach or pier,' said the signs. 'My god,' I thought to myself, 'what sort of place have we come to?' No dogs allowed all over the place or so it seemed, the only ones we had come across were the ones that have an urgent need to inflict pain.

On our way back to the relative sanctuary of the caravan park, we walked on the other side of the road to avoid our earlier encounters. One of the other caravan park residents was walking his small dog on our side of the road. We exchanged pleasantries and then discussed the benefits of walking on one side of the road. "I never walk along a nature strip or footpath where there are low fences, I have seen what's across the road and take precautions accordingly." That I could understand as his dog was one of the smallest poodles I had ever seen. One bite, one mouthful and the poor little thing would be gone.

Things did improve dramatically when we were driving down the road a short distance towards Urangan. We parked in one of those off-street parking bays that allow direct access to a variety of beachside picnic areas. There was an answer to our confusion as about dogs on the beach. Most of the beaches where we attempted to take Stan for a walk had notices all over saying, 'no dogs here.' We made our way over to the foreshore edge and noticed several other dogs on leads being walked on the sand. I said to my wife, "hey, come over and have a look at all this, bloody tourists ignoring the signs." I went a little further to the edge and you could have knocked me over with a feather, or even a full dog poo bag. 'Dogs permitted on leads' with an arrow to the right. That was enough for us. Stan was trying to eat his way out of the back seat of the car, one look our way and saw us come back to the car and the barking started. No matter how hard it is sometimes to do the simplest things, such as take the dog seat belt off the dog and put on the long lead for a walk, it's bloody difficult when your stupid dog is doing the following: yelping with excitement, spinning around in circles and trying to lick your face.

Before we headed north to follow the sun during our miserable winter, I made a long lead out of a six-metre length of rope. A clip on one end and a loop on the other. All this rope combined with the state of anxiety of our dog made for a particularly testing time for our morning walk. All three of us made our way to the concrete steps at the top of the beach. Stan took one look at what was in front and took off at speed. Luckily, I had looped the end of the rope around my wrist. Stan was airborne before he hit the sand. My wrist broke his surge for the sand, the fact that my hand felt like it had separated from the rest of my body was enough to think, "is this a really good idea or not?"

The things we do for our pets. Pick up their poo, walk them constantly and occasionally give them a brush. But one of the joys of owning a dog is being able to take them to a beach. Our Stan has an issue with other dogs. Being only ten months old now he has no concept that other dogs would prefer to eat him rather than doing a bit of bum-sniffing. So, off we went, ready to walk to the stone rock wall two kilometres off in the distance. The tide was going out, so the sand was easy to walk along. Others were finding their own pleasures on the water's edge. Several fishermen and ladies were trying their luck on a specific stretch of sand. Two small boats were anchored in the shallow water only fifty metres from the shore. Why on earth that location appeared to be the only site along four kilometres of beautiful beach where they were catching winter whiting, I will never know.

I have been known to dangle a hook or two off piers, jetties, and rocks, so it went without saying, I just had to have a sneaky peek into their large, white, plastic fishing buckets. To my surprise, most of the buckets were half-filled with seawater and contained several whiting. Absolute bloody tiddlers, after having to scale the little things, clean then remove the insides, I would have thought all the effort would have been a waste of time.

Was I a little envious? Of course, I was, so we continued along the sand. Several other dog owners were casually walking their dogs in both directions, and as soon as Stan noticed, the ritual began in earnest. At the end of his six-metre rope, spinning and doing pirouettes at the same time. Barking like there was no tomorrow, the only remedy was to reel him in like a massive tuna on a boat. When he was finally beside us still barking, the only thing to do was grab him in a bear hug on the sand and cover his eyes to obscure the sight of the other dog. My wife at this stage was apologising to anyone who would listen. "So sorry, he's only a puppy, he won't bite he just likes to say hello." Most owners, to their credit, understand our predicament and usually offer those kind and reassuring words, "we all go through it he'll eventually grow out of it." Great thanks for your advice and help. When we took Stan to the local vet for his injections, I asked him how long the puppy stage will last? "Well, Graham, he will be like this for at least two years." Both Karen and I looked at each other and thought, how on earth are we going to last the next two years?

Anyhow back to the sand. We were making headway towards the end of the beach when there in front of me were two empty, large crab shells. Stan raced over and began to eat one of them. Are crab shells with the remains of a bit of crab meat inside suitable for a dog to eat? With our luck, he would have eaten them, got a bit of shell stuck in his throat and needed to visit the local vet. I quickly picked both shells up and tried to hide them from his view. This of course was a futile thing to do. Our dog has one of the most magnificent noses known to the animal world. He can detect a discarded piece of pizza on the footpath twenty metres away. Two crab shells in my hand were a no-brainer. Now leaping in circles and barking incessantly, I thought this was all too much. I quickly turned around and tossed them both back into the sea. I hoped he had not noticed but I was wrong. In a flash, he took off for his first true bit of open-water swimming. Not that far, but enough for him to think, 'what on earth am I doing in this water?' The shells sunk to the sand aided by the small waves that were breaking on the sand. He retreated and continued his merry way. We finally made our way to the rock breakwater, touched the rocks, and then turned around.

It's interesting that when you turn around and return from where you have just come from the vista can be completely different. Was it the morning light, or was it just that we had completed half our walk and were on the home stretch? Although not in the tropics, Hervey Bay can sometimes give you a feeling that you are in a different world, staying in a caravan park two streets away from the beach is all well and good, but consider this. Hervey Bay was once a small and sleepy settlement but now the population is well over fifty-five thousand people. From my observations, the old and original settlement was only two or three streets wide at the most. Many of the older and original houses remain, but many are now surrounded by modern holiday developments. Even on the beach front many of the very old-style Queenslander homes still cling to their past.

When we looked back into the distance from where we were standing it did make us incredibly happy to have escaped the winter down south in Victoria. Constant news reports on national television were showing heavy snowfalls and gale-force winds. We on the other hand in the middle of August, were walking along the sand dressed in only shorts and tee shirts. A hat and sunglasses completed our attire.

Looking west, as that was the direction in which we were headed, more people were occupying our little slice of paradise. More anglers angling, I had to say that, and more walkers with their dogs all destined to come within barking distance of Stan. And so, the process of reeling him in, my wife apologising for his behaviour and then a bit of mutual bum sniffing from both dogs and then we were back on our way. This process continued for the next two weeks, and we both agreed, my wife and I, that all this exercise could be bad for us. A couple of days off were required to let our poor old legs recover.

Chapter 2

What to do and where to go? That was the question. Being secreted away among fifty-five thousand others we needed to get out of town and explore a bit of what the area had to offer. We looked at the maps, well really, I looked on Google Maps and then decided to head back west to the town of Maryborough. On our way into Hervey Bay from the Bruce Highway, there is only one way and that's through the once, regional town of Maryborough. Only thirty-odd kilometres from Hervey Bay but really in another world. History and both of us really appreciate any old towns and their historical backgrounds.

When we initially drove through on our way to Hervey Bay, we followed the most direct route as indicated on the signs. The last thing we needed when dragging our caravan through a large town at the end of a long drive was to go sightseeing and to come to a dead-end street with nowhere to turn around. As soon as we got closer to the centre of town, a brown sign indicated 'Tourist route.' This of course was too good to be true. Turning left where the sign indicated, we followed the now very faded brown tourist signs until the next intersection. "Where do I go now?" I asked my navigator, "I think there's something at the next corner at the traffic lights." Sure, enough as we turned right and headed into Lennox Street the quality of the homes dramatically changed. Gone were the old and decrepit houses that were lining Saltwater Creek Road that we had recently been on. It was like we had stumbled into another world. Stunning and beautiful old Queenslander-style homes. Beautifully manicured gardens, cool and lush in appearance. No two homes looked the same, I can only guess that when they were originally constructed, money talked. Prestige and location went hand in hand.

As the centre of the town came into view, so did the Brolga Theatre and Convention Centre on the left. Little did we realise that over the back of the theatre was the magnificent Mary River. Seeing the sprawling expanse of Queen's Park down on the left, the first thing to do was find a car park. We didn't know anything at all about the town, apart from what we noticed on our original drive-through, and that wasn't much. We needed a walk and so did Stan. We found the car park in front of the Convention Centre and we were off. Well, Stan was off and racing.

Being on his short lead didn't slow him down. He was ready and willing to be our guide and leader for the morning. As we made our way into the gardens, we were stunned by what lay out in front of us. Why hadn't we heard about these fantastic botanical gardens? We noted that the Queens Park in Maryborough is one of the earliest botanical gardens in Australia. Nestled beside the mighty Mary River, the area of a little over thirteen acres in the old terms is smack-bang in the middle of town. Heritage listed, the vast expanse of lawn, gardens and river views give the visitor a wonderful insight into the town's history. The closer we walked to the higher point in the gardens, the more impressive was the area.

The local council should be highly commended, as the area is one of one those special places that the visitor comes across occasionally by chance. High above the riverbank is a series of original grand buildings but looking at the flood marks on the side of the old Bond Store, not high enough. The measurements up the side of the building show a maximum height of a whopping forty-four metres. Years are shown according to the river height and without doubt, it is terribly difficult to comprehend how anything survived.

As we were wandering around the area, the local authorities were in the process of constructing a new floating pontoon. Eight huge steel black posts had been embedded in the river to allow for another of those massive floods. Black, with a yellow, fluorescent ring below a white cone-shaped cover on top. From a visitor's perspective, a real eyesore but essential in times of extreme floods.

I happened to notice a large group of visitors being taken on a guided walk around the historical area. The guide, dressed as the town crier, was speaking with a great degree of enthusiasm as most of those characters do. Standing on the raised lawn area beside the Bond Store, he appeared to be holding an antique firearm of some sort. Although the assembled crowd on the lawn had some idea of what was about to occur, it was only after a fleeting glimpse that I noticed the firearm being raised. We were standing on the lower section of the walk and didn't really have a clue what to expect. Without warning, a blast from his antique gun shattered the otherwise feeling of serenity that we were surrounded by. Smoke was seen wafting from the gun's muzzle. It appeared to be a percussion firearm of some sort firing, not a bullet, but a blank. With our ears copping the full force, we almost needed to pick ourselves up off the path.

Reading from the wonderful signage that is throughout the area, the town of Maryborough was established in 1847 and proclaimed a municipality in 1861. One of the features of Queen's Park is the little railway running along the riverbank. Run by the local railway historical group, the replica steam train, the Mary Ann, runs on the last Sunday of each month. By a stroke of luck, we were visiting on that Sunday. Half a dozen enthusiastic locals were thoroughly enjoying their activities. Two on the engine and another two on the three carriages. The remaining two were happily sitting under their blue marquee. One was selling tickets for $5.00 per adult and the other was happily answering any questions. We wandered over and were told, "would you like to take your dog on our train?" Well, that was a revelation, would we what? We purchased our two tickets, loaded Stan onto the carriage and then boarded ourselves. With the engineers messing around on the engine, black steam blowing directly over all of us, we departed on our little journey. We were an eclectic group sitting in our three little carriages. We needed to race to get aboard, well not really, they saw us coming and did the right thing as far as we were concerned. Our carriage was the first of three.

On board were several disabled people each with their own carers. The rest of us were obviously older tourists and a couple of young families. The Mary Ann trundled along the tracks beside the Mary River and through the gardens on the lower level. Not knowing what to expect and how far we were going to travel, we arrived at the end of the rails before heading into a supermarket. The stop was reached just before Sussex Street where a couple of people waved to others who were watching the whole event. So far, the journey was a bit of an anti-climax, as we had only been riding the rails for around five minutes. As the Mary Ann didn't have anything to link a turning basin, the engine was put into reverse and shunted back towards the makeshift station. Expecting to alight, we were surprised to continue backwards alongside Kent Street.

From the display information in the park, the area was a vast ship-building centre and, at one time, the busiest port in all of Queensland. During the second half of the 1880s, over twenty-two thousand people from all over the world arrived at the port of Maryborough as immigrants. I can only imagine the looks on their faces when arriving at the area. Firstly, arriving by sailing ship, then manoeuvring all the way up the Mary River and getting off and being confronted with such a place. Stuck in the middle of nowhere, a river that sometimes is home to crocodiles and so far from home. Even up to the Second World War, ship-building was a vital industry, but now the major industries are both sugar production and the construction of trains. One of the volunteers at the little station was proud to explain that the line that the Mary Ann runs on is still owned by Queensland Rail.

We continued backwards, past the old and now-disused buildings that were once part of the port industry. Right next to the massive derelict building is the only boat-building business still in operation. As with all good things, our little train ride returned to base and we all thoroughly all enjoyed our peek into the past, and even Stan was well-behaved considering it was his first experience of travelling in something other than a car. Five dollars per adult is great value even if we did get covered in a bit of soot. It all added to the experience.

Chapter 3

The town of Maryborough does seem to have found something to hang its hat on. Mary Poppins. Created by a local writer of the time, P.L. Travers, who was born in a room above a bank in the middle of town. Her father was the manager of the bank at the time. The historical area around the port and the old bank is portrayed as the birthplace of Mary Poppins. The quiet fact of the matter is, P.L. Travers only lived in Maryborough for the first eight years of her life. But let this not distract the visitor from the wonderful fact that the author was born in the town and is celebrated with a great degree of gusto. There is a magnificent bronze statue on the corner of the street just under the room where the author was born. Several large murals adorn the surrounding area. If we didn't read all the material explaining her origins, we really would have not stumbled across this wonderful display of affection for a totally fictional character.

It was a shame that she lived most of her life in England, both as a journalist and author, and is buried in St Mary the Virgin's Church in Twickenham, England. From what I have read, she led an interesting life; from having a relationship with George William Russell, the playwright, who was almost fifty-seven when he and Pamela, then a young twenty-five, got together, to being in a three-way lesbian triangle, it must have been one hell of a life, but good old Mary Poppins still has the appeal to draw in the tourists even after all these years.

When we finally ran out of things to poke around in Maryborough, we noticed a sign pointing to Tin Can Bay. The signs stated seventy-five kilometres and, having the afternoon free, we decided to head in that direction. The trip should only take an hour, so having not been there for many years off we went. We had no idea what to expect but it was near the water and that was our mission. Shortly after leaving Maryborough, a commercial pine plantation appeared on the right. Living in the northeast of Victoria, pine plantations are nothing unusual. The scale of these plantations in Queensland was indeed epic. For over fifty kilometres on both sides of the road and sometimes as far as we could see. One thing that did cause a bit of concern was several roadside signs warning drivers of wild horses. Horses and pine plantations, who would have thought this could be possible? There we were, driving along at one hundred kilometres per hour watching out for the odd wild horse and kangaroos. Imagine coming across horses on the road in the dark; large kangaroos and wombats we can deal with and even deer at home, but horses?

When the never-ending pine plantations finally finished, we found our way to the sleepy hollow of Tin Can Bay. I can only presume that the area must be one large retirement village. A small group of shops, a caravan park, a golf course and two lawn bowls clubs. Set on the edge of the water in an idyllic location, it's one of those places that would be in trouble if there was a rise in the sea water levels.

We have noticed in our time in these areas that for some strange reason the local authorities permit the development of residential estates in the strangest of locations. Tin Can Bay is one of them. Located on the right-hand side as we entered the town was a reasonably large residential estate out in the middle of nowhere. Speaking of nowhere, I would not like to have a medical emergency and need to be transferred to the nearest hospital. But some people love the idea of living away from the rest of the population and having the security of others nearby. Everyone to their own I suppose. We needed to escape, as my wife seemed to be suffering a big dose of sinusitis, possibly from the millions of pine trees by which we were surrounded. Back to Maryborough via the same road, but have you ever wondered why, when returning from somewhere, it never seems to take as long as the original journey? In this instance, thank god as we were back in Hervey Bay before we knew it. My wife did place a notice on Facebook, 'Tin Can Bay, never again, too many pine trees, not good for my sinus.' And that would be true, once was enough, but twice, we've got to be joking.

Chapter 4

The next bit of exploring, as there is a need to venture outside the city limits of fifty-five thousand, people was a short drive north to a secluded and real gem of a place. Only eighteen kilometres from where we are staying is the little settlement named Toogoom. Heading to the beachside town of Burrum Heads for a bit of a look around, we noticed a blue sign on the right-hand side of the road in the middle of a paddock. 'Take the second turn on the right to Goody's café.' And turn right we did, and we were absolutely delighted with what we found. Literally at the end of the road was the beautiful inlet on Beelbi Creek. Open to the ocean with access via the creek, the combination of sand, turquoise water and a beautiful café perched on stilts overlooking the water was too good to resist. To the left of the tiny car park was a selection of old original beach shacks next to multimillion-dollar houses. It was easy to guess the value of the properties as there was a block of land right on the waterfront with an old shack perched on the sand with a for sale sign asking for $750,000. Purchase the site, knock down the shack, build a house and then enjoy the privilege of owning such a property.

At the end of the road, was the café, gift store and, of course, a real estate business. Not knowing what to expect as far as finding somewhere to have lunch, we could not believe our good luck. There on the blackboard at the front of the café was a hand-written message in chalk, 'dogs welcome'. "A bloody miracle," I said to my wife, "you aren't going to believe this, the café is dog friendly." "Show me where it says that, and I'll believe you when I see it."

We entered through the delightful front of the café and were shown to a table overlooking the inlet. The staff were polite, courteous and well-versed on the meals available. Stan seemed happy as he immediately spotted another couple of dogs from his vantage point below the table. Our only decision to be made was what to indulge in for lunch. Already quite overwhelmed with the location, the sun was beaming down and the breeze soothing, it was time to order. I chose the barramundi, and my wife ordered the salt and pepper calamari. Both were served with a fresh garden salad, and those wonderful, large, crispy wedges. You know the type, the ones you cannot ever find the way to cook at home. Large, golden, and crispy. I asked for a beer while my wife ordered a vodka, lime, and soda. Stan, on the other hand, was quite content with a few of his dried dog bits and a bowl of water. As we sat there enjoying the view and the whole experience, we had a short think about what may be going on back in freezing Bright, and thought, 'well, no one's missing us, so let's be happy at this moment in time.'

It is wonderful being in contact with the rest of the world, but sometimes we all need a break. A lady sitting behind us felt the need to answer her phone with the loudest voice we had endured for some time, and then proceeded to let the rest of our fellow diners all about her family and friend's problems. I really did feel like saying, "are you really serious, we're all here enjoying lunch, turn your phone off." Of course, no one said anything, we all just pretended it wasn't happening. Did we all home in on her problems? Of course, we did, it's just human nature.

We lingered there for as long as possible, and then paid for lunch and wandered around the foreshore. Down on the water's edge, two men were talking. One was squatting down on the gravel, while the other was standing beside asking what he was doing. I, being naturally curious, couldn't help myself and went over to see what was going on. An old tinnie, for those who are not Australian, a tinnie is a small metal boat primarily used for fishing, had been dragged up onto the gravel and was secured with the anchor resting up a little higher. The man who was working on his catch appeared to be concentrating and didn't seem to like that attention. You know the type, salt of the earth, and intent on appearing to be invisible. I noticed that he was in the process of cleaning several very large squid. Stripping the outer skin off and pulling out the other bits and pieces that squid have. I am sure there are correct terms for all of this, but I haven't a clue.

If I had been in his situation, I would have been keeping an awfully close eye on the water. Deep and blue, and to the observer, it looked very much like crocodile country. Although there were no signs warning of the threat of crocodiles, the fact did spring to mind that we were in the 'croc area.' Toogoom is the small settlement at the end of the road that I have just been talking about. Only sixteen kilometres north of the massive Hervey Bay area, the region does have the odd croc around. A week before our staying in Hervey Bay, there were media reports that a large, five-metre crocodile was found and removed from the nearby Mary River.

The Mary River that flows through the nearby town of Maryborough finds its way to the ocean at the appropriately named town of River Heads. We drove south the short distance from Hervey Bay and had a quick look around the area. There was no way anyone should venture into the water as I would think no one could swim that fast to the other side with a reptile following them. I have often considered whether a fish or a bit of frolicking in the water is worth being eaten? I think not.

Back to the Toogoom area, million-dollar holiday homes on the shores of the inlet certainly did look very appealing. But when we are away on holiday, many places do have that appeal and we often wonder what it would be like to live in another place. Then we have a bit of a reality check, think of our family and friends back home and then dismiss the thought.

It was time to move on after our three and a half weeks living in our own little can of sardines. Our mission was usually to drive for around three and a half hours, maybe a little longer if needed. On this leg of our journey, we had planned to drive to the industrial town of Gladstone. A drive of a little over three hundred and fifty kilometres. For some amazing reason, we were all packed up and raring to depart before nine a.m. A miracle, as we usually forget to tie something down, pack some equipment in the right spot and then leave. All was done and dusted, I did all the external stuff like the awning, seating and caravan stays, winding them up and locking them away. My wife does a far better job of packing all those bits and pieces away inside the van than I could ever do. All we needed to do was hitch up the van and drive off north to catch the last of our winter weather.

Chapter 5

Hervey Bay and the surrounding fifty-five thousand population were obviously having a lie-in on this Sunday morning. Within ten minutes of handing in our electronic keys to the park reception, we had driven out of the surrounding area. I have always decided to fuel up the Ford Everest, or our previous vehicle, on the day before. Firstly, to ensure that the tank was full and, secondly, it prolonged the need to drive into the nearest town and avoid demolishing one of their fuel bowsers.

There is somewhat of a short-cut back onto the main Bruce Highway and this is through the tiny town of Torbanlea. From there we drove to the town of Childers. As I have mentioned earlier, we can usually gauge how a rural town is going by the number of visitors and locals milling about their main business area. Childers appeared to be booming. There wasn't a free car park in sight let alone a vacant shop. I can only presume that, being located on the main highway and a point on the road that is the centre of the region keeps this lovely part of Queensland thriving.

Our tentative goal for the evening, as I just mentioned, was the town of Gladstone. Due to the amazing fact that we got away far earlier than usual, we were sitting down and having possibly the worst cup of coffee in the world. This destination should remain a secret as all those who drag their caravans around would have the same level of disappointment as us. Suffice to say, the town begins with the letter G and is followed up with another G. We had taken Stan for a short walk around the park in the centre of town when it dawned on us, we would arrive in Gladstone early in the afternoon. "Let's see if the site we had booked at Kinka Beach was available a day earlier." With a resounding, "yes," we made the call and gave Gladstone a miss, maybe next time.

The day with a certainly proved to be a little longer and more arduous than we had hoped for. Towing our van for a total of a little over four hundred and fifty kilometres for a couple of old crackers like ourselves is a fair old effort. The Bruce Highway did make the journey a little easier, but still, we were glad when we reached the outskirts of Rockhampton.

As we recalled from our last visit to the region, the first thing that greets the traveller to 'Rocky,' as the locals refer to the town, is a magnificent, big, grey brahman bull statue. Not one, but two of the big buggers. One on the first major roundabout south of the town and the second one closer to the centre of the city. It really is the centre of the region, with a population of over seventy-seven thousand according to the 2016 Australian Census. Located on the magnificent Fitzroy River, where I should add, there was a large crocodile sighting where the locals had been water skiing before our visit. I can only assume, that an exceedingly high degree of skill would be required to have a go at water skiing on the Fitzroy River. Not a place for the raw beginner.

Chapter 6

Anyhow, back to the trip. It had been three years since our last visit to the region, and to be honest, nothing much seemed to have changed. The outskirts of 'Rocky' on the way to the seaside town of Emu Park appeared to be in an even more dilapidated state of decay than on our last visit. The two old hotels in the area around Kalka were closed and the housing was in a very poor state indeed. Not a good look, but these things happen. Driving along Lakes Creek Road on the way to Emu Park, a massive structure on the right of the road turned out to be Teys Australia. From a bit of research, Teys Australia is a meat producer in partnership with the Cargill Company. In conjunction with their partner, Teys is the second largest meat processor and exporter company in Australia. Even from our quick drive past the massive facility, the business is integral to the region, and Rockhampton in particular.

As we were driving along the now Emu Park Road, we were realising it had been a long drive and were looking forward to arriving at the Island View Caravan Park at Kinka Beach. When entering Emu Park from the west, the outskirts of this delightful town seemed pretty much as it was on our last visit. The gentle rise opposite the primary school leads to the magnificent view overlooking the islands of the Keppel Group. The water was, to use an Australian term, bloody brilliant. Turquoise blue, and hardly a breeze to disturb the vista.

Coming down the hill into the town, it's a sharp turn to the left at the first roundabout and then only six kilometres to Kinka Beach. All looked the same, the small police station on the left, and the caravan park on the right. The backpackers still seemed to be in business on the left, but I did notice that one of their small busses was now being used as a small school bus. Maybe this was just a bit of a convenience, or maybe it was the need to diversify the business.

Up the hill and out of Emu Park, with those luxury houses overlooking the Coral Sea on the right, our goal was in sight. A couple of kilometres, then the right-hand turn onto the Scenic Highway. Just a short way from the intersection is the strangest thing. Australia is known for its big things. The Big Prawn, the Big Banana, the Big Penguin, but on our visit, to the Big Penguin in Tasmania it wasn't really that big. Lots and lots of big things. Have you ever heard of the big whale? I would think not. Maybe down Hervey Bay way or down Warrnambool way in Victoria.

So, as we drive along, there he or she is. An exceptionally large whale. One of epic proportions. Sitting all alone on a large vacant block of land. On our past two visits, the poor old whale was in desperate need of a makeover. Immediately to the left with the whale strandings are the remains of a now derelict tourist attraction. By looking at the faded lettering on the building it must have been the site of a large aquarium and natural history tourist attraction.

From what I have noticed over recent times, these small local tourist attractions really are things from the past. Unless your business has a large and wide appeal, such as Australia Zoo, or even places like the Big Banana, which have expanded their businesses to cater for a more diverse clientele, these smaller attractions just don't seem to have the appeal as in the past. So, there we are, looking at a bloody huge, grey fibreglass whale sitting all alone next to a derelict building.

Well over five metres high, that was quite easy to presume, as the front lower section of the mouth is large glass windows and a pair of double glass doors. The area above this was about the same height. I had a look at Google Earth to see if the whale was visible. To my astonishment, it stood out like the proverbial. If you take the time to have a peek as I did, the whale really does appear to be the same shape and dimensions as a blue whale. I can only wonder what those boffins somewhere around the world would think if they were scanning this area of Queensland and the image appeared.

I can imagine there would be calls and emails to those who are fascinated with whale strandings. Fleets of volunteers could be sent in search of the beached, blue whale, trucks bearing signs saying, 'save the whale' and 'protect our planet from climate change.' would all be heading to the little section along the Scenic Highway to save the whale. The media would be in an absolute frenzy. Worldwide media coverage would ensue.

When all those parties arrived to save the poor whale, it could take a bit of time to comprehend what they were being confronted with. A large, grey whale, well at least it had been freshly painted, three hundred metres from the beach and sitting on freshly-mown grass. Oh well, maybe one day the entire site will be re-developed into a thriving tourist attraction again, but I have my doubts.

It was only a couple of minutes before we reached our destination for the next eleven nights. Island View Caravan Park sits opposite a magnificent stretch of sand and appeared to be pretty much the same as our previous stay. Still owned and operated by the same family, I was greeted like an old friend. "Well, that was a good start to proceedings," I mentioned to my wife who was trying to control an overly-excited Stan in the back seat of the car. We have begun to think Stan might have a bit of a psychological problem because of the sight and sounds of the ocean, or possibly anything else in his young life that gets his attention, be it other dogs, cars and people. We think he is stark raving mad. The constant jumping, spinning, and barking were driving us mad. We spoke to our local vet prior to our trip, and he said, "don't worry, he's just a puppy, he should be fine when he reaches two years of age." Great, if we all last that long, let alone in our caravan for eight weeks.

We paid the balance of our account and were directed to our site. Great, a drive-through site only two sites from the recently-renovated amenities block. It's always interesting when arriving at a new caravan park for a stay, and in this instance, things were no different. The eyes of all those already in residence, who were nonchalantly sitting back reading a book or working on their crosswords. I know for a fact that we were being watched as the odd glimpses were checking out the new-comers. It should have been a rather easy process of driving straight ahead for forty metres, turning left, then turn left again. By this stage, Stan was beside himself with excitement. Having been secured in the back seat for many hours, he was becoming desperate to get out and do what dogs need to do.

"This should be a breeze," I said to my wife. "I'll drive straight through, unhitch and we should be all settled in a couple of minutes." Famous last words. I feel like I've said that many times over the years. "I'll get out and look after Stan, just in case you need a bit of direction," she uttered. Stan at this stage was barking at the top of his range.

I lined up and proceeded to drive onto the site. Either side of our site were caravans and their awnings. Immediately on the right, as I was making my way onto our allotted site, and I should say, confidently, was the neighbour's brand-new awning. I thought there was more than enough space, but no. It was the scream of, "stop! You're going to demolish their awning." I looked in my driver's side mirror and to my horror, the front right-hand side of our van was only centimetres from their awning. I immediately stopped, and thought, 'thank god, that was a bit lucky.' I needed to reverse slightly without smashing anything and drive around again.

Around I went again, and I was sure even more of our fellow caravanners were watching my second attempt. Meanwhile, my wife was chatting with the neighbours on the left. It turned out that the couple on the right whose awning I tried to demolish only that morning had had the front driver's side of their four-wheel drive Mercedes smashed off. It seemed that the previous occupants of our site were not concentrating enough. I know from first-hand experience this is an easy thing to do.

Our site did have the benefit of having a concrete slab where the awning was. The caravan was resting on grass, so I needed to manoeuvre as close as possible to the concrete with my second attempt. There was no way I was going around again and to suffer the same embarrassment. So, it had to do, a one-and-only second try, that sounds a bit odd, but that's what was required. A miracle happened, things lined up, the neighbour's awning was spared, and the van was reasonably close to the concrete pad. 'Close enough for me,' I thought. A bit of a technical issue here. The van wasn't close enough to the concrete, but stuff it, it had to do. One of the Issues if a caravan is too far away from the concrete is the space between the two objects. It is quite easy to fall out of the van when there is no opportunity to place a step into the position. We always carry one of those small, grey plastic steps for this reason. Me, in my less than wonderful parking attempt, this time really stuffed it up. I almost needed to write us each a note and stick it under our noses to remind us to watch the gap. But I must say, for the duration of our stay, neither of us managed to fall out of the van, but Stan was confused for the first couple of days.

No damage was done to our neighbours, and that was both sides. I did catch a bit of a look at the poor old Mercedes. It was not a pretty sight. The elderly owner 'was busy applying a decent amount of builder's duct tape over the entire front right-hand corner of his vehicle. How it was damaged I am still to work out, but he didn't appear to be too fazed, but I can only presume he was parked in front of his van at a right angle. This does sound a bit like an oxymoron if that's what it's called. Maybe not really the right angle at all.

We then went through the process of setting up for the next eleven days. Our neighbours two doors down proved to be an interesting couple. From the Gold Coast, they had been staying at the Island View for a little over eight weeks. He, tanned, barefooted, clearly relishing his time in the sun and enjoying their retirement, while the lady of the manor, simply ignored the rest of the world and stuck to herself.

As soon as we had sat down, there he was, making polite introductions and telling us his life story. He and his loved one were selling up their relatively new 24' Jayco Silverline luxury van as he was struggling with the winding mechanism of the jockey wheel. Maybe he thought we may have been a couple of prospective buyers, but that was the last thing we needed in our lives. A monster van. There was a handmade for sale sign stuck on the four sides of his Silverline. 'Best of luck with that,' I thought, from general observation, lots of retirees purchase the biggest caravan they can afford at the time. When age and fuel costs catch up with them, many are trading in their vans for something smaller. Does that sound familiar?

He quite proudly mentioned that "we've already rented an apartment for eight weeks next year, so at least we won't miss out on coming back." 'Well, that's genuinely nice,' I thought to myself, but maybe you shouldn't have recently purchased a monster van as you did. Anyhow, back to what I was telling you about before I interrupted myself. It was nice to be back in familiar surroundings, or so we thought. This time, we were located between two access roads, but still in a good location. Close to all we needed in the park, and even closer to the beach than before. One clear disadvantage was that we were open to all those who wandered, drove, and sauntered past our site. A bit like being attacked on all fronts. There was nowhere to hide.

The novelty of being available to all concerned for a wave and a chat soon became less than desirable. I said to my better half, "should I put up the privacy screens on both ends of our awning?" "Oh no, they'll think we're being a bit snobby, just put up with things the way they are." The movements of cars and caravans, maintenance vehicles were never-ending, from early in the morning till early evening.

On our second day, while I was out walking Stan on the beach over the road from the park, I missed a terrible event that became very distressing to all who both witnessed the event and read about it here. As Stan and I were returning to the caravan park entrance, several people were talking in hushed tones, and a few were covering their mouths in horror with what they had just witnessed.

An older couple, it was not stated if they were staying at the park or were only visiting, didn't realise or probably forgot that their old dog was still on its leash while tied to the rear tow bar of their vehicle. My wife heard anxious screams coming from all around her while she was sitting in our caravan. It turned out that the dog owners were oblivious to the plight of their poor old dog who was being dragged along the gravel road and out onto the Scenic Highway. I did notice a vehicle pulled over on the side of the road a couple of hundred metres away, and I can only presume that was the vehicle in question.

Being a dog owner, I can only put myself in the place of those poor people and think what a traumatic event that must have been. Not only would you have to reconcile with what had happened to your beloved dog, but the shame that you would have felt about an old member of the family.

The next morning while I was making my way to the dump point, and for those who are not familiar with the term, a 'dump point' is the place in a caravan park in Australia where the contents of your toilet canister are emptied. Dump points come in a vast variety of styles and types. The stock-standard type that is usually found in most caravan parks is located away from the main activity area, down the back of the block, hidden away behind a screen of some type. Most are a large blue plastic hinged lid that sits over a white metal base with a large hole in the centre. Nearby is a hose attached to a tap to wash down the base when the contents of the canister are emptied. No matter how hard I try, there is always a lingering, small amount of liquid that finds its way out through some secret crack in the canister. It then invariably flows over one of my hands. I suspect I am not alone in all of this, but really, it's not the thing that springs to mind in normal caravan park conversation.

In other caravan parks we have stayed in, their 'dump points' have covered a broad spectrum of styles. One park that will remain nameless has a small sign wired to a fence above a modest plastic pipe sticking just above the ground. A bit like a submarine periscope jutting above the surface of the gravel. Another 'dump point' was simply a ceramic toilet cistern, sitting on the ground in the middle of the caravan park for all to see and use. The toilet does have a seat and a lid, and the idea is to lift the lid, if you are a man, lift the seat, and enter the contents of your canister into the toilet.

Others are grand affairs, some with lighting and soap in cute little dispensers, and one I visited even had a vase with flowers in it.

The emptying of the toilet canister is really a 'man's job.' Without the threat of being called a little sexist, in all our times dragging our caravan all over the place, I have never come across a female at the 'dump point'. A typical conversation goes like this. "Isn't it funny how we never see a female doing this task and it's them using the toilet most of the time?"

It was at the dump point that morning when I was witness to the following conversation by one of 'the others.' More about that shortly. "I would have tied that old fucker to his tow bar and dragged him along the road to see how he fucking liked it; wait till I catch up with him." I soon realised that the two 'others' were talking about the poor elderly couple and their now-dead dog. I do not doubt that they simply thought that the couple had done this with intent, but really?

The caravan park, when we had previously stayed, was home to several permanent residents living in either their own caravans or in small cabins that the owners offered for that purpose. On this visit, a section of the park overlooking the swimming pools and barbeque areas was now designated as 'private.' 'Please respect the privacy of residents,' said the signs at either end of the access road.

I acknowledge that there are many in our community that are not as fortunate as others and do have the need to find accommodation wherever they can. A couple of the residents do seem to be employed part-time in the caravan park as maintenance staff, while the others enjoy their lifestyle.

I did feel quite self-conscious at times when the permanent residents made their way to the amenities block, as the usual route was past the barbeque and pool area and then into the area where the caravans were located. It appears that most of the caravans are modern, expensive and luxurious, and really are homes away from homes. There was one resident who was still in the same location as on our previous visit. I clearly recalled that when we last stayed, our site was right next door to his. A large old caravan, with a solid permanent annex attached. His palm trees were still rustling in the afternoon breeze as was his bloody television. He, and he was an 'old cracker' as one of our sons would describe a person who seemed to be tone-deaf and elderly, was reliant on the occasional visit of a mate, and his love of the television. If we didn't have a tv in our caravan last time we could just open our window, ask him to open his blind and we could enjoy the racing channel and the footy at all hours of the day and night. It was good to see that some things are the same, but we were glad to be located up the other end of the road.

Chapter 7

There is always one destination that we needed to travel to for the day. And that was Great Keppel Island. Sitting off the coast of Kinka Beach, the island is clearly visible, and always having had an unhealthy passion for islands off the Australian coast, we just had to make the trip again. With a stroke of luck, we discovered that the ferry service that operates transfers to the island now allows for the family dog to accompany day trippers. As Stan had already overcome his trepidation about travelling on a steam train, there was another challenge ahead for him. We made our way to the Rosslyn Bay Ferry Terminal and purchased our two adult tickets, and one for the bloody dog.

We had previously stayed on the island many years ago and we were surprised to find the entire resort, well, barring a couple of buildings, completely removed. The beach was still the pristine beauty that it was, but that was about it. The old Hideaway Resort was still clinging onto the sand dunes, but there was a great deal of retaining work going on to secure the facility. We made our way up the beach and onto the stretch of buildings that are still offering a few services to the day-tripper.

Lunch was beckoning, and we tried our luck at the Hideaway Resort. Dogs were not permitted in the area immediately around the bistro area, which was fair enough, so I tied up Stan to the table on the grass area near the beach and wandered over to grab a menu. Even by our standards, it was a little early for lunch, so we ordered a couple of iced coffees and a serving of 'fresh' scones with jam and cream. A delightful young lady promptly delivered what we ordered and of course, offered that word that really annoys us of the older generation, "enjoy."

Well, the coffees were okay, it's not that hard anyway, but the scones were from a different planet. Possibly, Uranus. Scones, to the uninitiated, should be light and fluffy and be able to be pulled apart with a couple of fingers. These two little objects would not have been out of place in the Boer War. Whack them into a small canon and fire them off at the enemy. They could have perforated six-inch steel.

I tried to make light of the situation, but in hindsight, the fact that they were hard and inedible and even Stan had a bit stuck in his teeth. We left the scones hardening even more in the sun while the cream, that obviously had been extracted from one of those cream dispensers, was melting away in front of our eyes. "At least the jam looks fine," I said to my wife, who then replied, "I have to say something to the young lady when she returns."

"Don't bother, it's not her, fault she is only delivering what the kitchen dishes out'. I said quietly. Sometimes, we males should really just shut up, and in this situation, I should have done that. When the waitress returned and asked, 'had we finished, and how was the food' to which my better half replied, 'it was inedible not even dog would eat it'. 'Oh, ok thanks for that, I'll pass that onto the chef'. And with that we scuttled back out of the area and made our way beach along the foreshore to the only other option for lunch.

Thank God there was another place as it wasn't long before we had grabbed a seat under a couple of palm trees, and each had a cold beer in our hands. With another three hours before our return trip back to Rosslyn Bay, the café that we had now taken up residence proved to be just the thing for our situation. Lunch was ordered, and while we were waiting the thought came to me that there was a chance we will never be coming back to Great Keppel. We sat gazing through the coconut palms which were decorated with many large fishing floats and numerous bits and pieces that the ocean had heaved up onto the local beaches. It was at this location many years ago while we were staying on the island for a week that one of the adjoining buildings was the site of Derrick's Tea House. Being somewhat of a beachcomber myself, I clearly recalled the morning Karen, and I made our way along the same pathway from the resort and stumbled into Derrick's Place, as it was known. Down a short sandy pathway and up a couple of wooden steps to his front door.

A quite knock on the barely hinged flywire door, and a 'come on in, and welcome to my place' said a tall and tanned man in possibly his late 50's. No shoes, tanned legs from years in the tropical sun, and wearing an old Hawaiian shirt. One glaringly obvious striking thing was the object he was wearing on his head. At a quick glace the thing could be mistaken for half a split coconut turned inside out. Without doubt the worst attempt at wearing a men's wig I have ever seen. Well, there would be no problems getting a sun burnt head wearing that thing. I gave my wife a quick kick under the table, and whispered, 'don't look now but there's an animal on Derrick's head'. If looks could have killed that was her response.

We ordered our tea for two and two serves of scones, jam, and cream. All served in floral China cups and saucers and set on lovely lace doilies. Even after thirty-five odd years, those scones were the best ones that we have ever had the pleasure in eating.

The inside of the café was what would be described as 'Retro', but the whole experience was one of those things to cherish for ever.

We thanked Derrick for his wonderful hospitality and tried not to look at the animal sitting proudly up on top. It was next morning while we were walking along the beach after breakfast when we came across Derrick and his pet, and noticed he seemed to be at peace with the world. Sauntering along the shoreline, gently splashing with his feet in the crystal- clear waters of Keppel Bay wearing only a long pair of weathered shorts and his friend on top. I can only presume that Derrick is now making those delicious scones somewhere in the sky, but at least those wonderful memories remain.

Anyhow back to our predicament. How were we going to occupy the rest of our time on the island? I for one felt the need to wander around the outside of the security fence of the old resort. Stan was beside himself when I tried to leave unnoticed, but fortunately my wife managed to calm him down with our small supply of dog food that we had taken to the island for such an occasion.

As I made my way along the pathway that was partially covered in sand, I came to the crossing where the road that used to run along the side of the resort began. Turning left, the road that was once paved was in complete disrepair. Potholes the size of craters that could have been remnants of a bombing were all over the road. A couple of vehicles are still in the disused resort area and are used for the caretaking staff. As I made my way along the track, and that's what it now was, I glanced over to my right and there they were. Six lonely, unloved, small catamarans falling to pieces under the tropical sun. I would presume that one of them was the culprit that terrified my wife all those years ago. I know I have told the story in 'Life's too short to wear dull shirts', suffice to say, that was the one and only time my wife and I have ever been sailing together. Oh, the memories, and be perfectly honest, it was my last time in a bloody yacht, and thankfully the last.

As I wandered further down the track it was an incredibly sad sight to see the once proud resort in a complete state of neglect and decay. Hidden in the tropical scrub were the remains of staff accommodation, and other relics from the past. I stopped at the area that was still fenced off and could see the resort's airstrip through the broken bits and pieces. Goats were wandering over the airstrip where once, thousands of tourists, and that did include us, arrived on this once tropical paradise.

I reluctantly made my way back down the track and to the café and reported my findings. 'The whole place is a wreck, and overall, a great disappointment'.

'That's nice dear, glad you found what you were looking for'.

'It's about time we made our way back along the beach to wait for the ferry, so we can escape this place,' I said.

We were making our way back along the beach for our return trip, but there was no sign of our transfer ferry. "Oh well, let's sit down on the sand and wait for the bloody thing, I hope it hasn't sunk as we'll be here till tomorrow," I said to my fellow stranded beachcomber. We were sitting there, the three of us when Stan thought it was time to dig a hole, and more than a hole, it developed into a trench.

They say, every dog can dig a hole, but this was Stan's first try at a bit of beach excavation. Even I was impressed with what was happening in front of my eyes. We had him on his five-metre-long lead so there was plenty of potential to find the right site for a bit of a dig. We sat down and watched the proceedings commence. First, in a straight line heading for the water, sand was flying out between his back paws like there was no tomorrow. A channel was being formed about a metre in length and he stood and gauged his progress regularly. Time would not stand still for this little dog; he was a dog on a mission. As the digging continued, to our delight the ferry appeared from around the southern point of the island. "Thank god, we're going to be saved," I explained to my wife. I then did as all frustrated males do from time to time, I recorded my thoughts on my iPad. Even I find myself still laughing when I look this up on YouTube. If you are interested, type in Graham Badrock Great Keppel Island and have a quick laugh.

I didn't realise this until we were back in the caravan park, but Karen was secretly filming Stan and his excavation while I was willing our ferry to come closer and evacuate us from the island. She did the only right thing and posted the images of Stan on her Facebook site. Within a truly short time, there were over four hundred views of bloody Stan digging a hole, while on my page on Facebook, the grand total of twenty-four. There is obviously no accounting for bad taste. Only joking of course, but it does give an indication of what is important to others.

The departure time had finally arrived, and all three of us eagerly made our way to the gang plank that was resting on the beach. Stan took one look at where he was supposed to be going and dropped to the sand. I therefore needed to pick him up, and walk up the metal walkway, trying not to lose my balance with this bloody quivering dog in my arms. 'Good afternoon, sir, have you enjoyed your day on the island?' Asked one of those young, sun-tanned people who always appear to be over-the-top happy. I muttered under my breath that 'I couldn't wait to get off the bloody island, what took you so long to come back and rescue us?'

The eleven nights did pass quickly which is always a sign the stay was pleasant, but our time was up, and it was time to head back south, hopefully, to warmer times in Victoria. It comes as quite a shock to realise that you have become a number attached to a dollar, and this was never more noticeable than on the morning of our departure. Everything was packed away. I must admit when using a caravan, it's good to have a look in the mirrors of the car when leaving to notice whether anything is still there or lying on the ground.

With no possibility of leaving things behind, I managed to manoeuvre our car and caravan around the last coconut palm that I could have collided with, then we made our way out past the reception area. There were the three owners only two metres from us having a chat among themselves, not a look, wave, smile, 'thanks for staying' not a single acknowledgement as we drove out of their caravan park forever. Oh well, that's how it was, as we realised that our paths will probably never pass again.

Chapter 8

Enough of that waffle, there was the rest of the trip to enjoy. Or was there? I had noticed on the morning of our departure that our pocket rocket of a dog, Stan, seemed to have eaten something down on the beach before we packed up. Not once but twice. He had developed a liking for both oyster and clam shells. He was constantly picking them up in his mouth and crunching them as quickly as possible before we had the opportunity to intervene. While we were driving south, he was unusually quiet in the back seat of the car.

We didn't really give this much thought as we made our way back down the Bruce Highway heading for the small and quite lovely seaside town of Moore Park. Moore Park is located around sixteen kilometres north of the large and industrial city of Bundaberg. After having moved onto our site without too many dramas, it was then time to take Stan to the beach which was only a few metres from the caravan park. The park's promotional website states, 'located on over twenty kilometres of prime and pristine beach.' It certainly did justice to those words. Stan at this time appeared to have recovered and was at his lively best, leaping into the air with the agility of a performing seal.

We made our way along the sand and, to use a great Australian saying, 'feeling the serenity.' There stretched out either side of us was the unbroken ribbon of sand as far as the eye could see. There he was, the bloody dog, finding and eating more shells, we considered, maybe he might have been suffering from a calcium deficiency or was he just being a dog?

Eventually, we thought it was about time to return to the van and get ready for one of those peaceful nights in the van. We made our way up the small sand dune and came across the Moore Park Surf Life Saving Club building. Was there a lack of local members, who knows, the building certainly appeared to be in desperate need of some love and attention? Old and locked up with nowhere to go, or so it seemed?

Back at our caravan, Stan didn't appear to be remotely interested in his dog food that evening. Mmm what was going on, this was very unusual indeed as he would eat anything that had once been alive, cooked and put into a packet?

Although we both agreed before our travels Stan should sleep on the floor on his bed, that was it. No bloody way, thought Stan, and with the agility of an Olympic high jumper he simply took off from a standing start and leapt onto the bed. No matter how hard we tried to toss the bloody dog off, he returned with the agility of a greyhound. Needless to say, he won, and we gave up. I must add, this was quite early into the trip. For the sake of this story, this is where things get interesting.

After we had gone to bed, Stan jumped off and began to scratch at the door of the van. This usually meant he needed to go outside and answer the call of nature. "My turn, I'll go outside and wander around with him until he does what he needs to do," I said to my wife who was comfortably snuggled up under the bedding.

There I was, wandering around in the dark, torch and poo bags in hand, Stan on the short lead trying to have a poo. Suddenly, without warning, Stan found the spot and had the biggest dose of diarrhoea one could imagine. Ten thirty in the evening, pitch black and with the sound of the waves crashing onto the nearby sand, there I was pretending to pick up a good dose of dog diarrhoea. Not a great success I should add, but it had to be done. Back to the van, jump back into bed and try to sleep. Half an hour later, the same procedure as before. "Bloody dog, I'll go again," I said to my wife who I think was pretending to be asleep.

We began to feel sorry for Stan, he had that look in his eye, while we were both standing out there in the dark, he with a great dose of the Jimmy Grits and me thinking, am I really doing this? Dressed in boxer shorts, tee shirt, torch, and poo bags in hand, listening to the soothing sounds of the ocean and a dog farting and pooing like there was no tomorrow.

Back to the van, and the novelty was really wearing thin. I said to my wife, "next time you take him, I'm done." I did have a small touch of the guilts, but only for a moment. Half an hour later, scratch, scratch, "it's your turn, make sure you take a torch," were my words of support.

Being in Queensland at the beginning of September, the evenings were reasonably warm. I caught sight of my wife going out the van door, Stan struggling to get outside, her dressed in a short nighty, torch and poo bags in hand. This occurred twice more after my wife's expedition out into the dark. The fifth and last excursion out into the night was mine around three thirty in the morning. Imagine my surprise as I went out to support Stan, there was another man dressed in his dressing gown taking his bloody dog for a walk. Armed sensibly with a torch, dressing gown and slippers, we gave a mutual nod, which I think really translated into, 'what the fuck are we doing at this time in our lives?' and 'isn't there more to life than this?' He disappeared into the dark down near the lake, while I pretended to scrape the remains of Stan's diarrhoea into the little black plastic bag. This is exceedingly difficult if you comprehend that the torch must be held between your teeth, with a desperate dog straining on his leash, and you hoping no one is peeking through their curtains.

The next morning enough was enough we both decided. We contacted a local vet in Bundaberg and made an appointment for the early afternoon. Stan by this time seemed to have turned the corner. He still wasn't interested in his food but at least the diarrhoea wasn't as bad. When you are in this situation, with a dog with the runs and residing in a caravan, any small improvement is a blessing.

We made our way to Bundaberg and just made the appointment with minutes to spare. Stan had only been in a veterinary practice a couple of times before. Once when he was de-sexed and the other more recently for his yearly injections. Both these visits must have etched in his little doggy brain that it wasn't a natural place to be. We opened the door, and he hit the floor. All four paws were firmly placed on the shiny surface, spread out like a starfish. Without really taking any notice, we kept walking to the reception counter a couple of metres from the door. Little did we realise that Stan was sliding over the polished floor like an Olympic ice skater, graceful and sleek to his unwanted destiny.

A relatively young and likeable man, possibly just out of his university course graduation, opened the door and ushered us in. Stan by this stage in proceedings was not impressed, was it the smell or could he sense what all this was about? I lifted Stan onto the metal table, while the young vet began to ask all those questions as to what was the problem? We gave him our opinion and then the examination proceeded. "Please hold Stan firmly around his head and shoulders while I check his temperature." If a dog's look could confirm what I was thinking, he would have been quite happy to jump off the table and retreat to the car. As soon as the vet inserted the thermometer into Stan's backside, Stan looked at me with his big brown eyes as if to convey, 'I'm not sure about this, will it take long?' His temperature was within the normal range, so a bit of a probe over the rest of his body declared that "well, he seems to be in fine condition, and by the way, he does have lovely white teeth." Both Karen and I thought, 'well, that's a relief, we thought we would have to return to the caravan and give his teeth a clean.' Now really. His weight was spot on for a dog of his age so that was a relief. The outcome? $90.00 poorer, but we did have three cans of dog food that was supposed to be highly beneficial to a dog that had been suffering from the runs. Great, so off we went back to Moore Park Caravan Park.

Back at Moore Park, we settled back into our normal routine. After an afternoon walk along the beach, Stan seemed to be fine with no lingering effects of his visit to the vet. Dinner time was pretty much the same for us, a pre-dinner drink sitting outside under the awning, then a barbeque for our meal. Stan on the other hand was trying his new, low-fat, low-protein and low just about everything else tinned dog food. Tentatively at first then once he had decided it wasn't poisoned, he ate the rest. Within a noticeably short period, he was looking to find a way to escape and answer his call of nature. Thinking that his new super dooper tinned dog food might have fixed his bowel problems I confidently took control and off we went. Almost in the instant he was away from the van, a rumbling could be heard and then the explosion from his bottom. He gave me, that look again, as if to say, 'is this really happening again?' I went through the exercise of pretending to pick up what he had produced, but it was extremely difficult as the waste had the appearance and consistency of chicken soup.

I made my way back to the van and reported the details and then said, "I think next time it's your turn." And with that, we went back to the crossword that we had been working on together. An hour later but this time it was a little after dusk, so doing the right thing, off Stan and I went again for a poo in the dark. Well of course, that was only Stan, but you know what I mean.

Still with his dose of the runs, but now the process was preceded with a short, audible grumble, then dog fart, and a quick turnaround during the process to look at me again. At least I carried a torch and managed to avoid standing in his deposit, as we made our way back to the van.

We then came up with a plan. Any plan would do under the circumstance, and I said, "I think it's the bloody tinned dog food this time, they say you shouldn't change your dog's diet, so let's toss the rest of the tinned dog food out and see how he goes." We only needed to take him out one more time that evening, as I really think there was no way Stan would have anything left inside to blow out his backside. The next morning the sun rose over the Pacific Ocean, and it certainly had the makings of a great day. No more dog diarrhoea and Stan seemed to have recovered again. Thank God, as we were packing up and heading south to Kingaroy.

Chapter 9

Another miracle, we were on the road a little after eight-thirty in the morning, and the weather was unusually hot. A strong northerly was blowing us down the Bruce Highway. For those of you who don't drag a caravan all over the place, it's a lot easier to be driving with the wind behind you than the alternative.

Talking about the wind, there was an ominous feeling in the air. Off in the distance, it was either a large bushfire burning off in the south or a dust storm. Our route south was along the Bruce Highway until Childers where we would turn right and head towards the town of Biggenden. One startling thing was, we were now travelling southwest on the Isis Highway. A very topical name a few years back for all the wrong reasons. I wonder what the locals thought about all those terrible times a few years back having to live and work on the one hundred and fifty-odd kilometres of the Isis Highway?

As we made our way into Kingaroy, the temperature was climbing as was the speed of the wind. A dust storm of epic proportions had engulfed the entire region. Light brown and slightly threatening as we made our way into the caravan park that we had previously visited. We found our allotted site, and fortunately, it was a drive-through one which suited us perfectly.

I really don't know what is worse, setting up at a new caravan park in heavy rain or stinking hot weather with winds so strong they could suck the fart out of a camel. We began the task of unhitching the van, usually not a difficult thing to do. First thing is to pull the brake lever up to stop the van from escaping. Next, fit the jockey wheel then attempt to unscrew the two d-shackles from under the tow bar fitting on the car. At this stage, things were going reasonably well under very trying conditions.

It was only when I was attempting to release the two, heavy steel stabiliser bars that things got ridiculously hot under the collar. "Fucking things, let go you bastards!" I yelled as the wind, heat and dust were getting the better of me. Stan was under the control of Karen and all he wanted to do was get in the van and away from everything. My wife, on the other hand, remained in control while I spat the dummy big time. When these situations arise, you can guarantee that that time is when the fingers will either be crushed, or the skin is taken off. Sure, enough as I was attempting to remove the bars, I slipped, and the bars managed to slightly crush my fingers and remove a layer of skin off three of my fingers.

Finally, the two steel bars were released and so was the tension. I wound up the jockey wheel and released the rear of the car from the van. My wife then drove the car forward slightly so the van could be lowered into a level position. I, on the other hand, had regained a small level of composure and began to quieten down.

We then immediately levelled the van, unwound the caravan stays and then I politely asked my wife to go into the van and switch the air conditioner on so we could at least cool down. I, in the meantime, continued with the other tasks with the van; connected the water and necessary hoses, but didn't bother with the electric awning, as I was convinced if it had extended out, it would have been ripped apart from its housing in an instant. I quickly made my way around to the door and entered what I had hoped would be a cool, if not cold, oasis. The moment I was inside, it wasn't much cooler than the oven outside the door. "Haven't you switched on the air conditioner?" I asked my better half.

"Of course, it's on, doesn't it feel cooler to you?"

"Well, not really, what temperature did you set it on?" I asked.

"I thought twenty-four degrees would be about right, with the fan on low."

At that moment in time, I really thought, 'is this really happening?' I grabbed the remote control of the air conditioner, switched the temperature down as far as possible, which was seventeen degrees and put the fan setting on high.

It wasn't long before a sense of calm and coolness engulfed our small, little part of the world. Stan on the other hand needed to go out for his daily afternoon constitutional. A poop and a piddle, so off we went into the dust storm and heat of the late afternoon. It was moments like these when you must ask yourself, 'is all this really worth it?' Of course, it was, but we all must head home sometime, but the wind, dust, and heat, we certainly could have done without.

Suffice it to say we did survive the night and the next morning the weather had calmed down, just a little. One thing that did catch our attention on the morning news was the outbreak of several bushfires in the region.

Of course, they were southwest of Kingaroy, and in the direction where we were travelling that day. Our departure from Kingaroy should have been quite uncomplicated, exit the caravan park, turn left, drive for a couple of kilometres, turn right and we should be back on the Bunya Highway. Easier said than done. Without the benefit of a road map, or road atlas, we left that at home as we thought relying on our electronic world would be enough, we missed the turnoff.

Realising that we were heading for the town of Nanango, and clearly going the wrong way, we stopped, turned around and finally made our way back to the outskirts of Kingaroy. Like the parting of the waters in the Bible, there it was, a large sign on the left, pointing the way to the Bunya Highway. Past the Kingaroy Airport and finally back onto the right road.

Travelling south along the Bunya Highway, it wasn't long before we began to keep a lookout for bushfires in the distance. Although, I must admit it was difficult to determine what was smoke and what was the huge dust storm that was still engulfing the region. One clear benefit of our travelling on this route was the truly magnificent Bunya Mountains south of Kingaroy. Over on the left, as we were making our way, the scene was very reminiscent of the area of Mt Buffalo in the Ovens Valley. Tall and magnificent granite outcrops with sheer faces falling into the valley below. If we weren't on a mission to Goondiwindi for the night, we could have diverted to have a closer look. One problem was Stan. No dogs are permitted in National Parks, so maybe another time.

The drive was becoming one of an endurance test. A howling wind was propelling us south through the dust storm and the town of Dalby. On this occasion there was no need to stop so we powered our way through, thinking that we did not need to try and reverse park into a tiny site as we did many weeks ago.

Chapter 10

When dragging our caravan along the Moonie Highway the road was just as deplorable as on our previous trip. Except that this time we were on the other side of the road. One hundred and fourteen kilometres of being bounced and shaken was not a nice feeling, so when the small settlement of Moonie appeared in the distance it was time to stop and regroup.

Overall, our meanderings in our caravan we have always tried to be a little self-sufficient as far as our lunches are concerned when travelling from one stop to our next destination. On this morning, all that planning simply went out the window. Or should I say, in our haste to get back on the road, we simply forgot. We had had enough of the shaking and rattling, that was for sure. We pulled over to one of our favourite stops, the little Visitors Centre in the middle of the town. Clean toilets are inside, and a lovely, lady volunteer sitting inside to answer your questions. It does sound a bit like she was sitting inside the toilets, but no, she was behind the counter, invariably knitting or hand-sewing some small item. These items are for sale, and we have collected several items from the Centre over our travels.

As we were travelling south in the middle of September, things were a lot quieter on the roads. Not only was it the weekend, but the season for the Grey Nomads was well and truly over. Most had already begun the migration south a few weeks earlier. Trucks moving their loads mustn't have reached Moonie on this day, as there were none to be seen. During our past stops, you would be taking your life into your own hands when trying to cross the intersection to the roadhouse. On this occasion, I felt we could have dragged a table and chairs out from the van, sat down, and played a game of cards. Not a soul around, so much so that the lady in the Visitors Centre was in the process of shutting up shop, two hours earlier than usual.

We on the other hand were getting a little hungry. The time had just clicked over two p.m. and all three of us were in desperate need of a feed. I do admit that description does sound a bit crass, but that's how we felt. Leaving Kingaroy in the hurry that we did, we didn't take our own advice and pre-make our lunch. Stan was catered for with his dried dog food, but for Karen and I that simply didn't appeal. I suggested that on this occasion, she make her way over the road to the roadhouse and purchase anything that looked reasonably healthy and appealing. While I, on the other hand, would take Stan for a short walk into the area behind the Visitors Centre.

So off we went in opposite directions. Stan couldn't have cared less where he was going so long as there were a few trees to sniff and piddle beside while my wife was having her own problems over the road. Being confronted with a vast selection of fried food and a comprehensive menu, she found it hard to select. What we did end up with would not have been on any pages of any book that came under the category of, 'healthy eating.' Cold, fried food of any type is not appealing. My wife knew that although we had been eating healthy food over the past few weeks, I was in desperate need of a meat pie. No such luck on this occasion, no pies or sausage rolls, so the only thing left was to order one hamburger with the lot. She ordered a sandwich of dubious background.

When we both returned to the van, still the only ones there on the massive area of bitumen, only one of us appeared to be happy. And that was Stan. Needing to get out of the wind and dust, there was no way we would be sitting outside under the gum trees as we had done before. As soon as we sat down to devour our late lunch, the sight of what we were about to receive, which sounds like something from my distant memory from Sunday School, turned us off immediately. I don't think it was the quality of the hamburger or the over-stuffed sandwich, it was the combination of a long day, unhealthy food and sitting in the middle of a dust storm in the caravan. We both looked at each other and said in unison, "I can't eat this, it just doesn't seem appealing." I took both packages, went out into the dust storm and tossed the entire bundle into the nearby rubbish bin.

When I returned shortly, now with a swarm of flies trying to get in the van, my wife had found a few old dry biscuits, tossed on some cheese and tomato and that was our lunch. Well, it was getting close to two thirty p.m. now and we had almost got past the stage of feeling hungry after all.

From Moonie, it was only a lazy ninety-eight kilometres down the Leichardt Highway to Goondiwindi. Thankfully, we had the wind behind us now and it was literally plain sailing south. Hardly a hill in sight, well nothing compared with the Bunya Mountains that were now well and truly in the past.

The landscape could only be described as totally stuffed because of the ongoing drought. Paddocks and fields that three years ago were lush and green after heavy rains and flooding were simply, dust bowls.

Driving down through this parched and arid landscape, I did wonder how the farmers could survive. The fact that there wasn't a single town along this section of the Leichhardt Highway, so for those who were still living in the region, it must always be a long drive to Goondiwindi for all those essential services that we all take for granted.

Chapter 11

As we made our way into the outskirts of town, not much seemed to have changed in the three years since our last visit. The same array of businesses dealing with the local agriculture side of things, several of whom had large stocks of metal silos in their yards. Obviously waiting for a change in the weather and for the finances of those farmers to improve.

We turned left as indicated by the sign pointing to our destination for the night. On our two earlier visits, the caravan park looked fantastic. Lots of green grass around the sites and even a few token palm trees scattered around. The sites were the same, all drive-through but this time not a blade of grass was to be seen. Sand, gravel and stones had replaced this once-green oasis. Stan, when he was released from the confines of the back seat of the car, seemed to take one look at what was in front of him and decided this was no place for a pee. No trees, they had simply dried up and withered, and as for grass, not a blade to be found.

We began the process of setting up for the night but didn't bother with the electric awning as it would have simply been torn off the wall of the van for possibly the second time in two days. Caravans to me simply don't look complete without their awnings erected. Somewhere to get out of the rain, and in this case, out of the blazing sun.

We arrived just before four in the afternoon, when the rest of the caravanning world also decided to pull in for the night. One moment there were only a few of us taking a break for the return home in the southern states. Then suddenly the caravan park was almost full. I have always been interested in where others in our situation have come from and 'where home is.' One of the quickest ways is to grab a view of their number plates, and that is always a bit of a conversation starter.

"Oh, I see you're from Victoria, have you been on the road for long?" And that's usually how a conversation will start. Most people, and I know that's a bit of a generalisation, will give you the time of day and proceed to be your new best friend for the next five minutes and end up telling you their life story. While the minority will simply smile and grunt and that's the sign to infer, bugger off. It was the former in this case. An older gentleman, I suppose I am getting to that stage at the age of sixty-five, became my new best friend for those crucial five minutes.

It was enough to ascertain that he and his wife were on their way back home to Launceston in northern Tasmania having spent the last two months in a small caravan park a few kilometres north of Mackay. By the way, after having taken his advice and looked on the Internet, we too have booked four weeks there next winter. Of course, that was until the COVID-19 pandemic raised its ugly head.

Another night in the dust and dry ensured we made a quick exit the next morning towards the town of Gilgandra. The further we headed south suddenly the wind seemed to change direction. We had noticed reports on the television news the previous evening of the horrendous weather the southern states were experiencing. Cold, rain and even snow in the northeast of Victoria around where we live. We were hoping to miss all this cold weather, as I have always maintained, the older you get, the colder it is in Bright in winter. As we were now into the second week of September, spring should have been springing out all over the place. Not this time. The closer we travelled towards Gilgandra, the colder the temperature became. So much so, that when we drove into the caravan park, I got out to check-in, and it was truly bloody freezing.

On our way through, close to eight weeks earlier, the heat was almost unbearable, while this time the complete opposite. I jumped out in my shorts and tee shirt, thinking all would be good, raced into the reception and paid for the night. The same owner welcomed me as before, not much had changed. We made our way to our allotted site and started the setup process all over again. One thing, the first was to connect to the electricity and switch the heater on to thirty degrees and full power. No romantic ideas of sitting outside under the awning sipping a cool glass of wine or two.

I needed to take Stan out for his evening walk, "try not to freeze," said my wife. Off we went, around the perimeter again as before. The dodgy lot was still in position in their camp circle. Their bloody dog was still on the prowl, but thankfully still chained up to a tree. Making a quick entrance back inside the van and out of the wind and cold, we assessed our travels and began to think of home. It was only another two long days of driving but at least we would have our own creature comforts. Space, and by that, I mean our own personal space. No matter how well a couple can enjoy the benefits of travelling together, it is always comforting to accept that when home, there are things that can be enjoyed with others away from the confines of being in a caravan.

<h1 style="text-align:center">Chapter 12</h1>

Anyhow, that's enough of all that, I shall continue with 'the quest for the lost coconut.' I was thinking back to all those years ago when growing up in Cheltenham in the south-eastern suburbs of Melbourne. I have always been fascinated with our own family history, and by complete chance, I noticed an article that popped up on the internet.

My parents were married in early 1952 and were fortunate to purchase a small block of land on Norma Avenue in Cheltenham. At that time, the area was part of a development that was located on part of the Allnutt Family dairy farm. Little did I realise how coincidental and important that decision would be to me for the rest of my life. Since the 1880s there have been four generations of the Allnutt family living in Cheltenham and more importantly where I grew up. According to the bit that was on the Kingston Historical Website, the Allnutt family began the Cheltenham Creamery and Butter Factory back in late 1895 as part of a company float. The family originally purchased twenty acres near the corner of Warrigal and Centre Dandenong Roads to set up as their farm.

Where we come into the picture is the time after the family sold off most of the land. The Allnutt Family had expanded their land holdings to close to one hundred acres. This land parcel ran all the way from Centre Dandenong Road with the western border of Warrigal Road down to the old Mentone Racecourse.

My earliest recollection is of our family house being completed, well, of course, it had to have been, but I can still remember the roads being constructed, so it must have been not long after the land was sold for development. Over our back fence was another world. Old farmhouses, drays and many other relics of the farming history littered the over-grown paddocks. The old original farmhouse was still being occupied by the 'old Mrs Allnutt.'

A couple of times in my early teenage years, a mate of mine from around the corner would summon up the courage to knock on her door and ask if we could play a few games of tennis on her court. A normal size asphalt court with faded white lines and surrounded by a fence of chicken wire held up with timber posts, none of which were vertical. The other side of the fence was enclosed with old tea trees probably endemic to the area. The problem then arises if a ball was hit over the fence, it was goodbye ball as it was nowhere to be seen. We always went armed with several old balls found around the house as my parents were tennis fanatics. The matches were competitive as things were between teenage boys. The matches simply concluded when we lost the last tennis ball.

It wasn't long before the old farm was subdivided and the history with it. The reason I have mentioned this is in my early days, and possibly still while the Allnutt Family still owned the Cheltenham Dairy, I fancied myself as a milkman. Not a career to make my fortune, but something to earn a dollar on a Saturday and Sunday morning. I did wander along each of those mornings for several months until the novelty of getting up in the morning around four a.m. Those were the times of horses and carts and lots of horse shit to shovel before and after the morning's round. If you are interested in my account of those adventures, it would be best to refer to my first book, 'Life's too short to wear dull shirts.'

By a stroke of convenience, the old dairy was just behind the corner of Station Street and the old 'right of way' Cheltenham. The brick shop on the left-hand corner was where every Friday without fail, my mother would enter and pay in cash from the weekly household allowance, money for our previous week's milk delivery. Just two shops to the left is another brick shop that has been owned for decades by my wife's family and continues to be that way.

A stone's throw, well, maybe a couple of good tosses if you were young and fit, would place you at the front steps of the Cheltenham Youth Club Hall. This rather nondescript building was the scene of the legendary, Friday Night Dances. Believe it or not, in the late 1960s and even as late as 1970, this was the place to try and find a girlfriend or boyfriend. Dances were strictly controlled, as were the rules.

No pass-outs, if you left the building before the end of the first session, there was no way to sneak back in. Intermission lasted twenty minutes and everyone was ushered out the front door to the small patch of grass out the front. Talk about a hot spot for talking to the opposite sex, we all really didn't have a clue what to, let alone look one another in the eye. All the girls' and boys' ages were from fourteen to about seventeen. After that age, the local pubs were the place to be seen.

All the males were expected to wear smart 'casual' trousers topped off with a collar and tie and if possible, a jacket. The girls always wore reasonably tight-fitting dresses and were out to impress. I suppose not much has really changed over the past fifty years except male teenagers today wouldn't know what a tie was, let alone a jacket. On the other hand, some of the young women, girls of the same age today seem to enjoy wearing as little as possible.

When I mention the dances, none of this flippant stuff today, we were regimented into two lines, and then instructed how to do the 'Pride of Erin', the Fox Trot and, if things were progressing to a reasonable standard, the Rumba would be attempted. In each half of the dance, the real highlight would be the progressive Barn Dance. It was the only chance to have a quick thirty-second chat with a new partner before she moved along the line. If you were lucky, when the music ceased for the next dance, you might get lucky and continue talking with your partner. If she was not impressed with your attitude, appearance, or simply thought you were a dickhead, she would immediately scuttle back to the side wall and retain her spot in her group of girlfriends. Then you had the long walk of shame back to the other side of the hall and wait till the music was about to restart. Talk about a difficult time for a teenager. If you didn't have a girlfriend, then there was only one thing to do. Get up the courage to make the walk over to the other side where all the girls were sitting. This was easier said than done. Two things had to be considered. Firstly, would you be refused and then must walk back over to the boy's side or was the next girl in line a prospect for a dance?

Even after five decades, I still remember many of my mates at the time standing in the foyer or glued to the brick wall rather than face the daunting task of asking a girl to dance. There always seemed to be more girls than boys at those dances, so the best time to ask a girl to dance was when the progressive dances were announced. Maybe both the 'wall flowers,' and by that, I mean both sexes got up the courage to cross the floor and asked someone for a dance. If you were asked by a girl for a dance, it was like finding a great big gold nugget, they didn't come along very often, but when they did it seemed like heaven.

At the end of the evening, and it was usually around nine p.m. the doors were flung open and the final chance for a chat with a girl or boy was possible. Most girls were collected by their worried parents while the boys simply made their way home on their own.

My mate at the time and I would walk the few kilometres home after the dance, and occasionally I would grab a 'dink' on his bike. For those of you who don't know what a 'dink' is, it's when another person sits on the horizontal bar between the handlebars and the seat. There's not much space and it was bloody uncomfortable, but that's what we did. One night when we were making our way along Centre Dandenong Road, it must have been relatively late as there wasn't much traffic about. Well, come to think of it, there wasn't really much traffic about then back in 1970. We came across a car smash and it must have just happened. A car had smashed through a front brick fence and appeared to have spun around on impact and was facing the road. To our shock, a man was staring straight ahead and seemed to be dead. His mouth was open, and his face was as white as a ghost. Not knowing what to do, we hesitated for a few seconds, then suddenly the lights at the front of the house were switched on and then we decided it was time to head home. At the age of fifteen, this has remained with me all my life. We never did hear what had occurred and didn't even mention this to our families, such was the shock.

The interesting thing about the Friday night dances at the Cheltenham Youth Club Hall, was, unbeknown to me, my future girlfriend and now wife was one of those young females sitting on the other side of the hall. If I had only realised that all those years ago, we could have met a few years earlier than we did and saved an awful lot of trouble.

Chapter 13

I was going through a few bits and pieces that my mother had given to me recently, you know the type, old photographs, sacred family mementos of long-forgotten family picnics and gatherings. One thing that especially caught my attention was a couple of my high school end-of-year reports. Having completed my form five year, and for those who are too young to know about these things, it's the equivalent of year eleven today. To say I wasn't that academically gifted would be an understatement.

Growing up in the 1950s and 60s, unless your family was focused on being one of the high achievers and you were expected to continue to university, most of the population attended school to find a job. A lot of my friends left school after year ten to either follow a trade and become an apprentice or for the girls, it was into a clerical field. I was somewhat pressured to at least finish year eleven and then find a job.

To prove to you that the situation regarding my scholastic achievements was below par, I will quote you the following.

Year ten end-of-year report, most of the comments from my teachers appeared to be constructive, for example, 'he would have achieved better results if he tried harder.' The one that really caught my attention all these years later was for science, in which I thought I would have done quite well, 'without doubt the worst student in my class.' It's quite an achievement when you think about it, I cannot imagine any teacher in this climate of political correctness saying such a thing. Today, it's all about positive reinforcement.

The parents would be up in arms and threatening the school with legal action. I have absolutely no recollection of my parents' response, but I can only presume that they weren't remotely interested as they were preoccupied with their own lives at the time.

I don't think I really comprehended what my future would be towards the end of my time at Cheltenham High School. Back in the early 1970s, there was no such support as 'Careers Days' and associated support from specific teaching staff. I couldn't wait to leave school, and because of my family's outlook on life, there was no thought of following a tertiary path.

It really felt like, 'go get a job and leave us alone.' Upon reflection, I am sure that wasn't the case, but when you are a sixteen-year-old male, you really don't have a clue about much at all. I know that I wasn't cut out to be a milkman and had been a male check-out at a local supermarket and that didn't seem to hold too much promise, so what was I to do?

After some soul-searching and a couple of interviews, one with the Commonwealth Bank and the other with a local sign company. a future as a sign writer was ensured when I was the successful applicant for Briner Ads new apprentice. I really didn't even consider it back then but was I the only applicant or were there others who applied? I settled into the mundane task of being the 'general dogs' body' to a disparate group of sign writers. I have already mentioned this story in 'Life's too short to wear dull shirts' but in this case, it allowed me to begin saving for the most important thing in my life at the time. A car.

There was a fair bit of pressure in 1972 for the day of one's eighteenth birthday to have the morning off and go and get your car license. In today's situation, a young driver, and let's face it, there aren't too many older members of the community who don't have a license, are expected to have one-hundred and twenty hours of supervised driving before attempting to sit for their probationary license. In 1972, all you had to do was book into the local license testing place, have a quick chat with the tester, and then jump in a car and try not to run into anyone while still observing the road rules.

In my case, there was no way my parents were going to put themselves in mortal danger and teach me how to drive. "Well, Graham, if you want to learn to drive, you'll have to pay for your own driving lessons through a driving instructor." And that was the end of the discussion. I found a driving instructor through the Melbourne Yellow Pages.

For those of you who are far too young to know what the Yellow Pages were, they were the massive, old books delivered to every household in Melbourne. Running into hundreds and hundreds of pages, with every known commercial listing known to man. The first task was to heave the book onto a table then scan the front index for the relevant category, find the page and then trawl through until you found what you were looking for.

Then it was your turn to ask to use the telephone. "What do you want to use the phone for?" And "make sure you're not too long, it costs money you know," said my mother. Always looking to save a few cents for their next holiday. Sometimes there would be no answer, and back then, answering machines had not been invented, so the process was repeated, "please may I use the telephone again?" And the same reply would be issued.

I booked my first lesson with the driving instructor. I recall very clearly the look on his face when he turned up for my first lesson. A look of, 'here we go again, how long is this going to take this long-haired chap to get his license?' I made polite small talk, as I was clearly mortified with the prospect of learning how to drive with a stranger.

I was ushered into his nice, white, small Cortina sedan. This was my first time sitting behind the wheel of any vehicle let alone with the key in the ignition. I had been instructed by my father, "make sure you learn to drive in a manual." To my now seventeen-year-old brain, I thought I was going to learn in a car, not by looking at a car manual. So, in I get, waiting to be told what's what. He patiently went through the essentials; key, start, brake, and clutch and, most important of all, the indicators.

"Ok, Graham first make sure the car is in neutral." 'What was neutral?' I thought to myself. Neutral found, then I was told to start the engine. "Check your mirrors" well, they all looked there to me, then "with your left foot depress the clutch pedal, and then very gently with your other foot push the accelerator a little bit." Things were beginning to happen. The engine was revving with the speed of a jet engine, and so was my heart rate. "Now take your foot gently off the accelerator and at the same time, slowly lift your left foot off the clutch." I did what I was told and then immediately the term, 'a kangaroo hop' sprung to mind. A great amount of energy was generated to move a couple of inches.

"Now Graham, this time I'll show you how it's supposed to be done." I switched on the ignition and, as if by magic, the car began to slowly move forward. It took me a few moments to realise what was happening. It suddenly dawned on me that the driving instructor had an identical set of pedals on his side of the car. It was then that I could feel how things were beginning to work and wasn't long before I was beginning to get the hang of this. Or so it seemed. Another couple of kangaroo hops when the instructor thought I was getting ahead of my ability. Then the inevitable question at the end of my first lesson when we rolled gracefully to the front of 1 Norma Avenue, "how many more lessons do you think I'll need?" I asked. Thinking just a few more after my wonderful first time behind the steering wheel, I was somewhat disillusioned with his reply. "I think at least half a dozen more then we'll see how you're going."

And so, it went on for the next six weeks, but on these further expeditions around the industrial area of Moorabbin, they were on a Thursday morning and time was given to me by my ever-accommodating boss, Brian Smith. Leaving the confines of Briner Ads where I had been employed as an apprentice sign writer was a daunting proposition. Trucks, cars other assorted traffic made those mornings a lot more stressful than leaving from home.

After my now seven lessons, the time had come for the big day. I had been booked into the Brighton Police Station where the license test would be taken. This required a drive of twenty minutes through the industrial area and onto the main road that ends up in Melbourne. Nepean Highway, back in the early 1970s was still busy, but nowhere near as chaotic as it is today.

We both went into the office at the allotted time, and then my instructor had a quick chat with the tester and then left the room. The idea was that I had a certain amount of time to get as many of the questions correct, then progress outside and take the 'real driving test.' The tester gave me the thumbs up, and said, "Graham, you have just passed the minimum amount of answers, so let's go and see how you can drive."

I thought at the time, 'well, that's a bloody relief, the driving test should be a breeze.' Wrong. Things were going well, the tester was sitting beside me in the passenger seat, while my instructor was sitting behind him. I did all the basic checks, but apparently didn't look in my revision mirror. "I'll ignore that, Graham, but remember that in the future." Off we went, through intersections, around shopping centres and back almost to the police station. Now comes the big one. "Pull over to the gutter and have a go at a hill start, Graham." I managed to do all the right things, didn't stall the engine, and gracefully took off up the hill. At this point, I thought, 'I have this driving thing in the bag.' One more task was the dreaded reverse parallel parking. "Ok, pull alongside this car on our left and reverse into the space behind," said the tester. Even to my eighteen-year-old brain, the space was one that I had no idea how to reverse into. My experience with the instructor had been limited to reverse parking lessons, in large vacant areas of asphalt.

Then the only objects that were in my way were a couple of bright orange witches' hats.

After my first attempt, which was a bit of a disaster as I began to mount the gutter, I was given one more opportunity to reverse back into the allotted space. This time I did manage to avoid mounting the gutter, but when the tester opened his side door to check if I was legally close enough, the gutter that I had thought I had neatly nudged up against was a metre and a half away. Fail, no license that day, but just to finish off the ignominy of my experience, the instructor was now in the driver's seat and on the way back to the police station with me firmly in the back seat.

I wasn't allowed to drive back to Moorabbin, as it was deemed that I needed a few more lessons. When I sheepishly arrived back at work, I briefly mentioned that I "just missed out on my license, it was only a technical issue" that was when the rest of my fellow workers saw through my ruse and asked about the details.

Another two lessons later, we were booked into the same police station and went through the same procedure as before. By some strange twist of fate, the earlier bookings were running overtime, so my driving test was cut short. The same tester was in the seat on my first attempt, so he had some idea of my reversing skills. We quickly went through all the motions as previously, but when the time came to reverse again, he simply asked, "have you been practising your reversing, Graham?"

"Of course, I have, several times." "Well, in that case simply drive back to the police station and we'll process your license, congratulations, and remember to watch out for those gutters." And that was the beginning of the rest of my life.

I had been diligently saving for the past twelve months and my parents thought hard and long about what car I should buy. The result was a 1962 blue Volkswagen Beetle. This little car would open a wonderful opportunity for me and my new girlfriend to explore life together.

Chapter 14

A family favourite was the Sunday trips up in the Dandenong Ranges east of Melbourne. Only an hour's drive from the family home in Cheltenham, but another world. It was with a great big dose of enthusiasm that both Karen and I invited our then friends from the Mentone Tennis Club for a barbeque up in the Sherbrook Forest. A map was handed out for the location of the Badrocks' special place in the hills. This event was the catalyst for several future visits to the area. Not during the day, but for a couple of evenings at the well-known Baron of Beef.

On one less than memorable trip, we had all left the Mentone Tennis Club straight after our afternoon matches for a night of frivolity and great entertainment. The Baron of Beef was one of those iconic, themed restaurants that were extremely popular in the 1970s. The magnificent old guest house named Marybrook had been renamed and re-badged to become Baron of Beef.

Situated on a quiet and secluded part of Sherbrook Forest, the building itself resembled an extremely large mock Tudor mansion. My very first recollection of the magnificent building was several years before this evening. On one of those many Badrock family barbeques up at 'Sherbrook,' we were made to wander for what seemed hours through the forest and past this building. I really thought at the time there was no way any of the Badrocks could possibly afford or could enter through those magnificent front doors.

The magnificent building was originally constructed in 1940 as old-style English Hotel. Constructed over three stories, plus the small attic rooms in the roofline, the building came across to us as a place of unimaginable luxury and class, certainly no spot for the Badrocks. Or so it seemed. How times had changed when our group of eight drove up to the front gates and entered another world.

Pristine gardens, fantastic water fountains, and a bloke wearing a kilt standing up on the terrace, all combined to ensure the evening was one to remember. By the way, the man in the kilt wearing the complete outfit of a

Scottish piper was there not only to set the scene for the evening's festivities but also to play a pivotal role in the later proceedings.

Jack Farr and his family, who were the owners and operators of the Baron of Beef at the time, created one of those 'themed' restaurants that were so popular in the Dandenong's at the time. Others that our family and friends had the opportunity to enjoy were the icons such as Fiddlers Green and The Cuckoo.

We were on our way to the Baron of Beef, it was a reasonably long drive through the south-eastern suburbs and then into the foothills of The Dandenong Ranges. I was with my new girl-friend in the front seat and another couple was nestled quietly in the back all making our way up through the forest to Kallista. From that point, it was only a short distance after Grant's Picnic Ground and the turn left onto Sherbrooke Road that things began to get a little more interesting. When I look at the view now via Google Earth there was only one bend of any substance. The bend in question is a sharp right-hand turn that nearly ended the night before it had even begun. Trying to keep in front of the other two cars that our friends were travelling in, I maybe took the bend a little too fast. Upon reflection, driving the old 1962 Volkswagen Beetle, the brakes were not designed for a bit of rally driving. At the last moment, my driving adventures seemed to be all over in an instant. A quick, short and rather desperate shove down on the brake pedal, resulted in us sliding into the vertical embankment right in front. We were now in darkness and staring closely at a large tree fern that had appeared out of nowhere.

The James Bond, 'shaken but not stirred' quickly came to mind. The others following, slowed to see if we needed a push, and seeing that everything was okay, took off and disappeared around the next bend. The evening was one of those to remember. Being the Baron of Beef, all the staff were dressed in clothing that now would be described as sexist and demeaning. All the female staff were wearing extremely short skirts and even shorter tops. The colour scheme was green skirts, red tights, or as they are called today, leggings and the short shirts were white. The ensemble was completed with small red hats that you could have expected Robin Hood and His Merry Men to have worn. The male waiting staff were a little more conservative, dark trousers and white fluffy shirts and wearing the same hats as the female staff.

Upon entering through the dark heavy wooden doors, it was really like going back in time to the Tudor period in England. Dull, and the lighting was even dimmer, with lots of dark timber panelling being the setting for the many old English shields that were mounted on the walls. Who knows, they might have been real, but on the other hand, they may have been plastic.

As we were shown to our tables, the bloke in the full Scottish attire was seen lurking outside the front door. As soon as the guests had all arrived and the signal was given, in came the procession. The Scottish piper first, followed by the host, Jack Farr, and then in descending order all the floor staff who were on duty. It may seem a little dated and a bit twee, but it was the 'in thing' at the time. Themed restaurants were all the rage back in the 1970s.

As the evening progressed, so did the parade of themed courses. First, the entrée, usually soup accompanied by a white bread roll, then the main. The main course was not for the faint-hearted. Before the current fashion, or should I say, the fad of every third person being vegetarian, the main meal consisted of the following; roast beef smothered in rich, thick gravy, a liberal dose of peas, roast potatoes and pumpkin. All this plus the ubiquitous Yorkshire pudding.

Of course, one of the highlights was the welcoming of 'The Baron of Beef'. Four of the male waiters proceeded to carry the cooked meat through the dining area to the cheers and applause of all the diners. Not just on any old plate, but a large solid timber platform that was hoisted onto the shoulders of the four men. Very spectacular and this all added to the excitement for the evening.

When all this was served by the Maid Marions, the diners were serenaded by the resident band in the dance area. The music, although dated at the time, was a fantastic hit with all those there. Songs like, 'Do the hokey pokey, put your right foot in and turn around,' and such were great fun and most of the diners got off their seats and joined in.

While all this frantic activity was taking place on the dance floor, the tables were serviced ready for the true highlight of the evening. At the end of the musical set, "ladies and gentlemen, please resume your seats and we'll be back after our break." We all knew what was next.

Dessert, not any old boring fruit salad and cream, but the real deal. Using the same large timber board that was used earlier for the roast beef, four young, and usually attractive women carried in the dessert. Always eight, tall plum puddings were ceremoniously paraded into the dining area. Warm brandy had been liberally splashed over the top of the puddings and then set alight. With the lights dimmed again the pudding parade made its way around the dining room. Everyone's attention was fixed on the purple-blue vision that was before them. As the flames diminished, the puddings disappeared back into the kitchen to be cut up and plated. Presented to all diners, no questions asked, what more was there to do than begin the glorious task of eating freshly-cooked plum puddings covered in a rich brandy sauce?

As the evening concluded, most of the diners made their way back outside and invariably it was freezing as we did so, but there were a few lucky ones who had booked into the attached accommodation. We only had the privilege once and I'll get to that later.

The Baron of Beef was to become a favourite for the Badrocks and several evenings were enjoyed with both Karen and my parents. Not together but on separate occasions. We were not married at these times, and the Badrocks and Munros, as far as the parents were concerned, didn't appear to have much in common. It always seemed to be a bit of a balancing act when they were together.

On one occasion still talked about, well between Karen and I was an evening at the Baron of Beef with my parents, Joan and Bert. My father did seem much older than I feel even today. You know the type, a man of his generation. Solid, devoted to his family and job. Thirty-five years working for the SEC. State Electricity Commission for those who might be too young to know what it was. I have always believed that 'he married well,' as they say.

Suffice it to say that he enjoyed the trappings of being married to my mother. They travelled extensively through their married lives and always seemed to be jetting off to exotic places around the world without their children. I suppose it was their choice, but we didn't suffer too much from being left on those occasions with a variety of odd ladies who were given the responsibility of caring for me and my two siblings.

The reason I have just mentioned all this is to say that, on the return trip from the Baron of Beef that evening, my mother's guard was down. More than a few glasses of 'Mc Williams Cold Duck' had been consumed, and by the way, that strange, cold, red sparkling wine was all the rage in the mid-1970s. As we were passing back along Centre Dandenong Road beside the Moorabbin Airport, a cry of, "I think I'm going to be sick." My father was still on a mission to get home as soon as possible. "Open the window," and with that instruction, she wound down the window and heaved all that good old Baron of Beef mixed with plum pudding straight out onto the road. It was a strange sight, but the amazing thing, nothing was said of the event till many years later. One of those things that disappeared into history but dredged up with the anchor of time.

Back to our other visits, both Karen and I made the way up to the Dandenongs and the last time was just a few months before our wedding. New Year's Eve with the outlaws. In truth, Karen's parents. Joan and Ken, always at war with each other or so it seemed. Ken was even older than my father in both age and attitude. A bit of a self-made man and one of those high achievers in his later life in the business world. Unless he was in the garden, he seemed to have one of those old blue blazers, or jackets which completed his attire. Always quite generous when we really needed a bit of financial support.

On this evening, we made our way up to the Dandenongs and to the Baron of Beef. New Year's Eve with all the bells and whistles as they say. But the big thing was Ken had generously decided that all four of us would be staying the night upstairs in the old accommodation wing. No en-suites back in the mid-1970s, just a few Men's and Ladies' bathrooms and toilets down the hallway.

I have two remaining photos of that night all those years ago. One of me wearing one of those funny paper hats in the shape of an upturned ice cream cone with a whistle stuck in my mouth, and looking like it had been a really, long, but enjoyable night. While the other is of my future father-in-law.

Jacket and tie, cigarette in hand and a very bemused look on his face. It was as if to say, should I keep up this façade or just let my hair down a fraction? On top of his head was one of those cylindrical paper hats in the shape of a French Foreign Legionnaire. I still recall all these years later that it was a night to remember. Later that evening when we were all tucked up in our own rooms, were there any late-night frivolities? Well let's say, 'what goes on at the Baron of Beef will stay there,' will you ever know? I don't think that's likely.

Chapter 15

As with all good things, it was time to move forward and back into the future. I had been recently made an offer that could have been too good to refuse. My youngest son, Doug, had been pestering me for the past couple of years for him and me to go fishing down at Paynesville. We had been extremely fortunate a few years ago to purchase a holiday house at the lovely, yet secluded destination on the Gippsland Lakes.

This was in the middle of December 2019. On our trip across Mt Hotham and into East Gippsland bush fires were raging north of the town of Bruthen. On our trip via Mt Hotham, would you believe it, we were driving through half a metre of freshly fallen snow. The day prior, the Hotham Road was blocked due to snow, while at the other end of the Great Alpine Road it was blocked to through traffic as a large bush fire had crossed the road north of Bruthen. It just goes to show how diverse our countryside can be in the space of a couple of hundred kilometres.

As Karen and I made our way up the mountain from Harrietville, it was obvious it was going to be a slow trip over Mt Hotham. Light rain gave way to heavy fog. The higher we travelled the thicker it became. The area known as Mt St Bernard was crawling pace only. Almost a white-out. Headlights on and keeping to the right of the red snow poles. The yellow line in the centre of the road was all we could see. Snow appeared without warning. One moment fog then the next instant snow all over the sides of the road. Fortunately, winter was long gone so it wasn't settling on the road, but earlier that morning a snow plough had pushed the snow to the side. So much so that close to the area known as the Diamantina Hut the snow was close to a metre high on the side of the road.

It did feel rather surreal, driving over the mountains in the first month of summer and being as cautious as the conditions would allow. Finally, the stone tunnel that denotes the entrance to the Mt Hotham Resort was reached. Almost immediately the snow and fog began to clear, as that side of the mountain has a southerly aspect. It was difficult to comprehend that once the resort area was passed, it was clearly visible that there was a large bushfire burning away far off in the distance.

The usual amount of traffic was making its way along the Great Alpine Road. It wasn't until we reached the isolated small town of Swifts Creek that the magnitude of the fires had become apparent. Over towards the east and it did seem far away, smoke could be seen gently rising into the sky. Swifts Creek did appear to be its normal sleepy little self with a few fire vehicles ambling about. No real sense of danger, so we continued further along the Great Alpine Road and headed towards the town of Bruthen.

The closer we drove to Bruthen the more the fire path had been obvious. On both sides of the Great Alpine Road, the bush was burnt through. It's a strange feeling when the driver is confronted with a scene of such devastation. All incredibly quiet, with all the undergrowth and the lower sections of the trees completely blackened by the fires. The occasional logs were still smouldering, but the threat seemed to have abated. That was all well and good, but much more about the situation later.

We managed to stay for several days to escape the summer crowds that were descending on Bright for the Christmas season. But, and there is always a but, we needed to return earlier than we really intended to do so. Families are strange creatures, as I have always explained to our, now-adult children.

The fires appeared to be almost out in the Gippsland region, so we returned over Mt Hotham to the hustle and bustle of Bright. "Hey, Dad, how about you and I have a night or two over at Paynesville and I'll show you how to fish?" There was no point in refusing this truly kind gesture, as our son, Doug, had been trying to get me into his bloody 'tinnie' for the past couple of years. A week before Christmas, over we went again, just he and I. Bonding, I think it's called. On this trip, these bushfires were looking ominous. Several fires had been ignited by a band of lightning prior to our trip. Once up on top of Mt Hotham, out to the south, or in this case, off into the distance on the right, the huge plumes of smoke were rising from the tinder-dry forest.

Did we turn around and return home? Of course not, we were on a mission to catch a fish or two. Eventually, a little after seven forty-five p.m. the remote on our garage door was flicked and we entered the safety of our holiday house in Paynesville. A short walk to the Old Paynesville Pub for dinner finished off our long day. I was expecting a bit of a sleep-in the next morning after the drive over the mountains. Wrong. "Dad, I think we should be on the Mitchell River, no later than seven a.m."

There I was at the age of sixty-five, thinking of a long sleep-in, well, at least nearing seven a.m. would have been wonderful. No, up and showered soon after six a.m. A quick bowl of cereal and a cup of coffee and we were in the garage ready to depart. Fortunately, Doug is rather good at reversing the vehicle and attaching the trailer to the tow ball. As soon as he reversed the car into the garage with the use of the reversing camera on our Ford Everest, something struck me as rather odd.

As I went to wind up the jockey wheel, you know, those small winding devices that are attached to caravans, trailers and boats that allow the trailer to be raised. Or lowered. There wasn't one. "Hey, Doug, where is the jockey wheel?" "Well, when Hughesy and I rebuilt the trailer for my boat, we just didn't bother attaching the old one, as I didn't think we needed one." Brilliant, what was I to know, but the one thing I did know with my experience with our caravan, is things are a lot easier with a jockey wheel.

When the Ford was reversed into position, a little in front of the trailer, the time came to lift the trailer and the bloody tinnie onto the tow ball of the Ford. Unless you have had the misfortune to do this in your own life, it would not be a highlight to remember. Both the Tinnie and trailer would have to have a combined weight of a couple of tonnes. Then, when at the correct height, attempt to drag the bloody trailer to the tow ball.

When all this heaving and puffing was completed, the garage door was closed and it was time to drive off into the wilds of the Mitchell River. Doug did consider launching his mighty craft at the nearby marina, but common sense prevailed, and we drove a few kilometres to the area known as Eagle Point. Eagle Point is a strange area. A few kilometres from Paynesville with a population of a little over a thousand residents. Two small caravan parks, a primary school and not much else. The one redeeming feature is the proximity to the shores of Lake King and the Mitchell River.

We entered Eagle Point and took a sharp turn to the left and entered the boat ramp. It did strike me as strange that there wasn't another vehicle or one with a boat trailer in the area. Were we too early or was the weather worse than what was predicted? Strong winds had been forecast for the afternoon for the region, but according to my captain, "that shouldn't be a worry, Dad." I have noticeably clear recollections of having the same conversation with my father many decades earlier.

Without any fuss, the boat and trailer were reversed back into the Mitchell River. It was quiet and the water was calm, but was it the quiet before the storm? You'll just have to wait and see. "Ok, dad, you just hold the rope and don't let go of the boat." Now it was being called a boat, which was a little refreshing. As we were ready to leave the safety and security of the little jetty, I made sure we were both wearing our approved life jackets. All was fine as I had taken the precaution of swallowing a seasick tablet prior to our departure.

Being a cautious parent, I enquired about the safety equipment. "Do you have an anchor?" "Yes, dad," and "how about the safety flares?" "Yes, dad." "Can I have a look at the flares as I haven't ever seen them close up, only on tv when those soccer idiots set them off at the football?"

So, there they were. Two packs of emergency flares, two colours as required according to the boating regulations. "Can I have a look, Doug?" "No worries," said the captain. I had a close look and there was a use-by date on both packets. "Hey, Doug, it says these are slightly out of date by only a week, does that matter?" "They should be okay for our trip this morning, but thanks for checking, I must buy a new set before I go out again."

As we made our way out towards the mouth of the Mitchell River, I must admit that it was not long before we noticed the breeze. The closer we got to the end of the Silt Jetties, as the area is known, the louder the wind appeared. Being reasonably sheltered at that moment there didn't appear to be anything to be concerned about.

After what seemed an eternity, the banks on either side of the river began to separate like the parting of the waters in the Bible. Out in front was the vast open expanse of water of Lake King. The water now appeared to be a match for the inside of a washing machine except that we were about to be tumbled into the suds. I don't know whether Doug sensed my fear of what lay ahead, or common sense prevailed. "I think this looks like a great place to drop a line or two," said my captain.

"Do you have an anchor, or are we going to drift aimlessly all over the water?" "Don't worry, dad, I'll switch the electric motor on when I stand up and I'll be able to steer away from the reef." I heard myself saying, "What! There's a fucking reef and we just going to wander around with your foot on the pedal of a tiny electric motor to steer us away from danger?"

Being the caring father that I am, the only thing to do was not say a word and follow instructions. I certainly didn't feel the need to stand up in the bloody tinnie, let alone cast a soft plastic lure into the wind to locate a suicide bream. I was presented with one of the precious, lightweight rods already fitted with a soft plastic lure resembling some type of dead fish. "You'll love the rod and you should be able to catch a few lovely sized bream," said my captain. I remained seated and cast my line off into the now dark and ominous-looking black waves that were surrounding the boat.

After a short period, the fish were not jumping out of the water and into the boat. We apparently could see them bunkered down on the sea floor. He had one of those wonderful pieces of electronic wizardry, an underwater fish finder and depth sounder. That's all well and good, of course, but we were on a mission. After fifteen minutes or so, it was time to move on to a quieter section of the river.

A quick flip of the electric motor back onto the deck of the tinnie and we were heading back to where we had come from. At least the river surface was calm. Not that serene but at least away from the now-howling gale that had swept across the lake. "I know another couple of great spots where I have fished before," said my captain. After another half an hour of motoring at the required ten knots per hour, we passed our original departure point. I did notice with a degree of satisfaction that my Ford was still there and appeared to be untouched.

As we made our way towards the large riverside area known as 'The Bluff,' it was time to have another attempt to find the elusive bream. "That looks like a great spot, Dad, I can see the fish on the fish finder, so we'll have a crack here for a while." "Sounds good to me," I replied. Up he stood, flicked the switch on the electric motor and we were off once again. Casting furiously like there was no tomorrow. To my astonishment, a fish took my son's lure.

'Well, bugger me,' I thought to myself. Is this the only fish in the entire river that had come up for air and swallowed his lure? The action was intense if only for a moment or two. The fish thought, 'fuck this, I'm off,' and with that, he or she headed straight for the nearest snag. Gone, but not forgotten. I can only presume that if the fish was ever caught, the lucky angler would not only have the joy of landing the fish but the added benefit of collecting another $25.00 fishing lure that would have been firmly wedged in the fish's mouth.

Talking about his lures, it wasn't the first time we had gone through the 'bloody snags, I've just lost another $25.00 lure, life's not fair.' Each time this occurred, I did think quietly to myself, why are you casting so close to the bank and those snags?' I did know the answer as he did mention it constantly. "The best place to catch a bream is where they live. Right under those submerged logs and near the riverbank."

I could clearly hear the traffic on the nearby road, but at least the wind seemed to have abated. Next stop, upstream towards the area known as, 'The Grassies.' After the first three hours in his tinnie, the novelty was beginning to wear a little thin. At least the river was calm, and my seasick tablets seemed to be doing the job. We once again decided that the fish were under the boat, and all seemed well. Several more fast and furious casts and not even a mosquito bite was had.

The decision was made to return to a new area that Doug had heard about on the local fishing website for the area. The area known as the 'Cutting' was our next target. Another forty minutes back down the river until almost back at the boat ramp. Did we turn back to the ramp? Of course not. Rather than turn to Starboard, I found the nautical term on the Internet, to the ramp, no, we turned left or as the correct term, to port to an area that didn't look too flash.

The area immediately out in front of us had a strange surreal appearance. Many dead trees, half-submerged in the water, and the odd appearance was completed with two extremely large, concrete water tanks in the middle of the water. Considering that the land either side of us was over two hundred metres away, I concluded that only in recent years there must have been a bit of a flood. Originally the area must have been a farm of some type as the depth sounder was showing relatively shallow water.

The further out we motored, the more dangerous the conditions became. Shallow water, strong winds, submerged trees and a couple of large old derelict concrete tanks completed the scene.

"Ok, Dad, I think this looks like the place to have a few casts," said Doug. He once again stood up, lowered the electric motor into the water, and with his foot controlling the motor, casually cast into the nearest tree. I, on the other hand, sat at the front of the boat, one hand firmly holding on like there was no tomorrow, and the other attempting to cast into the wind. To my surprise, and especially Doug's, I found my rod being attacked and bent over. Had I snagged one of his $25.00 lures? No, a fish of epic proportions had attacked my lure and was making for the safety of the nearest submerged log. All the while Doug was issuing instructions while still trying to control the electric motor. "Tighten the drag, don't let it get away, wind faster, it seems like a monster." Of course, you can guess what happened, the wind was now blowing at almost gale-force conditions, we were in a state of turmoil, and I was almost a hero. The boat was now being blown to the northern reaches of the area, and the fish managed to break the line and escape to the safety of its mother.

With a look of complete sadness, well, not really, I was happy to have almost caught one but after five hours the novelty was beginning to wane. Back at the boat ramp, it was decided to return to Paynesville, have lunch then, "have another crack." 'Great, can't wait,' I thought to myself.

After our quick break for lunch and the necessary toilet stop, it was back to the boat ramp to relaunch into Mc Millian Strait where most boaters who are in the Paynesville area put their boats in. A large concrete flat area open to the elements but in the centre of the boat building and repair businesses. Two ramps are for general public use so there wasn't going to be an issue of waiting for others to toss their boats into the water. I need not have worried about that in hindsight, as the weather was terrible. Howling winds and now white caps on the water. Our mission according to my captain was, "I know a couple of great spots among the canals, and at least we'll be out of the wind." 'Great,' I thought.

There were approximately four hundred metres to motor before we entered the main entrance to the canal system. Close to a hundred waterfront homes, and I must say, some very luxurious ones at that, snuggle up the man-made canal system. The majority of which have the essential, large and 'look at me' boats moored on their own private jetties. Speaking of 'look at me,' as we were motoring around those beautiful homes, one male owner conspicuously made his way out onto his deck, hitched up his trousers, put his hands on his hips, and peered our way. There we were motoring around slowly, in front of his castle and his luxury boat, pretending not to notice his antics. 'Wanker,' I thought, but given the chance, I would have swapped positions in an instant.

Anyhow, back to our tour of the rich and wannabees. As we were motoring around the canals looking for likely spots to cast a few dozen times, it struck me how fortunate a lot of people are in Australia. Although

Paynesville and our town of Bright are approximately the same distance from Melbourne in both kilometres and driving time, they are worlds apart.

Bright, as I have mentioned previously, is becoming saturated with tourists, fair enough as we were originally one of those. But in Paynesville, there is a vast cross-section of society. Dozens of luxury waterfront homes, and from what I observed, many had the appearance of being holiday homes, to older style, original seaside places that are barely habitable. The town has slowly developed into two halves, both commercial areas face the delightful waterfront, but really appear to struggle economically. There are, of course, the usual busy times of the year; Christmas, New Year and the Easter break. Apart from the odd long weekend, the surrounding area relishes being in its own cocoon.

As my captain and I made our way through all the canals, it was decided that a very fishy-looking spot had finally been reached. He jumped up with his usual enthusiasm while I remained seated at the front of the boat. Several frantic casts later, we both came to the same conclusion that the fish were not biting that afternoon.

"Ok, Doug, I think we have explored all the opportunities here, it's time to head home and make a pizza." All was going well until he left the canal system and entered Mc Millian Strait. After our six hours of motoring and the lunch break included, the weather now had become interesting. Interesting is a nice word to describe what we were now confronted with. Waves close to a metre high, smoke from the bushfires off in the distance and howling wind. Doug's little tinnie really was very well-suited to motoring around the canals, but not for what was in front of us.

As we turned right, or as the boaties call it, starboard, we both became drenched in the fifteen minutes it took us to return to the safety of the boat ramp. "Hey, Dad, I think we should drop the boat back and return to the harbour and try a bit more fishing off the jetties, what do you think?"

"Thanks, but no thanks, there is only so much fun I can have in one day, Doug, maybe next time." Being an excellent executive chef that he is, the menu for dinner that night was not fish, but homemade pizzas. A good way to end a long day on the water. Oh, well at least I would be having a leisurely breakfast the next morning before the drive home to Bright. Wrong on both accounts.

Chapter 16

Up early the next morning with the news that the Great Alpine Road had been closed due to an increase in bushfire activity. The alternative? A quick breakfast jump in the car and then head west along the Princess Highway to Melbourne, drive through Melbourne's Freeway system and then travel onto the Hume Freeway north and turn off just before Wangaratta. Then a leisurely eighty kilometres back home to Bright. What would normally take just under three and a half hours from Paynesville to Bright, had now taken us seven and a half hours with a five-minute stop. Was I getting too old for all this? Possibly.

Fire activity was becoming a normal inconvenience to us living in Bright. We had endured four major fires over our twenty-eight years of living in Bright. The fires that were started by lightning in mid-November had shown no interest in abating. The novelty this year was really beginning to wear off. The Government authorities felt compelled to issue bushfire warnings and updates on a regular daily basis. Which, of course, is all well and good, but sometimes things are portrayed as being worse than there really are.

The fire activity became a State-wide issue in early January 2020. Fires were raging in far east Gippsland, up in the High Country and particularly in our region. Lightning strikes were the culprit in most cases. Although there was no one to blame, we really thought 'why us again?'

A public meeting was announced, and most of the locals attended the Bright Event Centre. There was standing room only, and all the local and State emergency services were in attendance. There's nothing like an emergency to draw the locals together, whether it be fires or the occasional flood.

At this time, I think we all wished for flooding rains as good old Dorothy McKellar said in her famous poem, 'I love a sunburnt country, a land of flooding rains,' etcetera. There we were, over three hundred souls all waiting to be told if our lovely town of Bright was going to be burnt to the ground. Having been through all this before, as I said earlier, the procession of well-meaning, important people at the front of the room, maybe things were going to be a bit more serious than we thought.

Representatives from the Victorian Police, State Emergency Service, Parks Victoria and the local Country Fire Brigade. Toss in a few 'important' people wearing their Community Liaison Officer and Community Welfare Officers' vests, and the group was complete. Each took their turn explaining the current situation and the whole theme was, evacuate before it's too late.'

So, all of us, well, almost all, decided to pack up and evacuate first thing the next morning. "Leave before it's too late as the Great Alpine Road could be blocked at any moment." We had heard all this before, but due to both our sons and their families and our daughter leaving, there was no option but to join the exodus. Where to go? Considering we had our dog, Stan, with us so that did limit our options. Our caravan was sitting idly out the front of our bedroom, and although I didn't think of that option, my wife and neighbour, Rachael, both suggested, "why don't you take the van?"

Decision made, off with the caravan cover, tossed that inside the front door then wandered around thinking, what next? Will we be away for a day, a week or even longer? All the essentials were packed, clothing that we most probably would not need, food that was left in the fridge at home that would probably still go off in the caravan fridge and a bottle of wine or two that wouldn't go off but would be opened in case of an emergency.

A quick call to my sister down the road at Baddaginnie, which used to be a bit of a stopover when the old Hume Highway passed through, but now a real country backwater. More of a place where unless you had a relative living there, there would be no reason to ever drive into the place. From our perspective, twelve kilometres south of Benalla was far enough to escape the smoke and the ever-present threat of fire.

The town's claim to fame of now having two sets of post boxes standing forlornly out the front of the now- closed store. Well, not closed all the time, as the building now is the local opportunity shop open for a couple of hours per week. A little further along is the local CFA shed. For those who are not familiar with that, it's the local volunteer Country Fire Association. Directly opposite is the community hall and that's about it. One feature of this now-defunct place is the main Melbourne to Sydney dual railway line that slices through the settlement. According to the recent Australian 2016 Census, the population stood at three hundred and thirty-eight. The average age of the residents was forty-nine, and out of the population of three hundred and thirty-eight, eighty-eight had never married. It is that sort of place.

It was our place of safe refuge for three nights, and if we really wished to never be found, Baddaginnie was the place to be. During our drive from Bright we had the constant threat of bushfires in our rear-view mirror as we drove down the Great Alpine Road and turned left at the Hume Freeway. Smoke was everywhere, visibility was poor, and the roads appeared reasonably quiet. Maybe the rest of the world was escaping also.

As we drove off the Hume Freeway at the sign to Baddaginnie, we really didn't know what the future held. My sister had a large open area in front of her garage which suited us. Reversing with the caravan attached was no problem. Sometimes this can almost lead to a divorce, but on this occasion, the reversing gods were with me. A set-up of the van went as smoothly as I could have hoped, although the heat was extreme, the northerly wind was blowing and my wife was inside my sister's house with Stan.

Although the smoke was still about, at least we could see across the dirt road into the farmland in the distance. Thankfully, there wasn't a fire warning for the area, as it would have really been serious. Dry and withered grassland as far as the eye could see. A large clump of grey feathers was scattered on the ground in front of the van. "Hey, Meredith, what's with the remains of the bird?" "I don't think it was one of my cats as they don't seem to have the killer instinct, I think it must have been a fox." I for one was more concerned about her recent encounter with a large black snake at her rear door.

Although the remains of the poor bird were nowhere to be seen, it looked like feathers belonged to one of the two local guinea fowls that had been seen terrorising my sister's cats. When thinking about all this, if the murder of a guinea fowl had occurred in Bright there would have been hell to pay. Facebook with all the community going-ons in Bright, 'someone's something' would have needed to be accountable. Vigilantes would be on the prowl looking for the culprit. Then, those wishing to save the fox would be mounting a defence for, 'save the fox.' While in downtown Baddaginnie no one really cared, it was just part of the ebb and flow, almost like my sister's neighbour a couple of houses away who has a horse and a pony.

Not so different when you think about it, but this chap, and I did say a quick 'hello,' keeps his large brown horse, that sounds like it should be in children's book, and a small white pony in the paddock across the road from my sister's place.

What's so different about this? I hear you say. Each morning and late afternoon he can be seen leading his two horses to and from his carport to the paddock. He has converted his carport into two stables. Talk about liking his horses, one clue could be the old and now-discarded trotting buggy propped up against the fence. I can see one bonus with this type of pet, at least you would have a constant supply of manure for your garden.

In making mention of gardens, I couldn't see much evidence of gardens in downtown Baddaginnie. Maybe it was the lack of town water supply, or possibly no one could be bothered. I took Stan for his morning walk around my sister's area, and to be honest, the area reminded me of the housing in the Pacific Kingdom of Tonga. The only thing missing was the family graveyards out the front of the dwellings. Some dwellings seemed to appear to be liveable but only just. As I was wandering around, Stan and I came across a large shed that had seen much better times. Instantly we moved closer to the boundary of the property, two large and powerfully built dogs of dubious background tore out from the front door and proceeded to bark furiously at us. At the same time, the lady who was the resident roared out, 'get back here and shut the fuck up!'

I was about to say hello but thought better of it as even Stan could detect that we could have easily been dog food. Still shaken by all this we continued around the corner and noticed another large white dog standing guard at the front of another property. For all intentions, this looked a bit of a worry. It wasn't until we edged closer that we realised the dog was a statue. Stan still couldn't understand why the dog wasn't responding. Even so, Stan veered off to the right on the other side of the dirt road just to be safe.

After our three nights of safety, it was time to return home to Bright. Reattached the caravan, said our goodbyes and drove off into the bushfire smoke. An hour and a half later, we were back home in Bright. The town still had the appearance of a ghost town but with the added benefit of having a large contingent of Australian Army personnel driving around the streets. The smoke was just as intense as before our evacuation, and the Government Authorities were still issuing warnings. It got so bad that only after a few more days, the warning was again issued, "evacuate before it's too late as the Great Alpine Road will be closed again." We erred on the side of caution as all our adult children were going, so off we went to the wilds of Baddaginnie again.

The word had gotten out that, if locals were leaving again, it would be best to travel via Wangaratta and register with the Red Cross. I left my wife and Stan in the car while I made my way to the Relief Centre at the Wangaratta Performing Arts Centre. As we had the caravan attached, it was difficult to find a parking spot anywhere near the centre of Wangaratta. The only site large and long enough for our car and van was down near the Wangaratta TAFE Centre. I almost needed a cut lunch and a map to find my way back to the Relief Centre. Eventually, I found the place and waited in line to register our family's plight. The Red Cross members were all volunteers who had come from near and far to assist with the relief effort. Courteous and polite, but I must have appeared a little over all this, as I soon became the focus of a lovely lady with a badge on her dress stating, Wangaratta Pastoral Care. Never having been confronted with all the Government and media concentration like this before, it did take a while to accept that we needed to evacuate.

After registering, it was suggested to all who had done so, that a bit of financial assistance was available, so we were directed into one of two rooms. I was quite surprised by how many people I recognised from Bright, Wandiligong, Porepunkah and Harrietville. People who I sort of recognised from our local community were all drawn into this situation because of bloody Mother Nature. Lightning strikes all over the North-East of Victoria had tossed all these people into the same boat. The feeling was rather surreal. People you maybe would not have anything to do with in normal life were only too willing to exchange their thoughts and chat about the 'bloody fires' and the emergency services.

Six rows of chairs with about ten seats in each row. The idea was to sit the furthest away and, as the people who were attended to, the first row made their way to one of the four Government officials, we all jumped up and moved crab-like along the line. Food and water were offered by other volunteers and the time did drag, but what else was there to do?

Not having been in this situation before I didn't know what was in store. A Government hand-out in the form of financial assistance was available to those who had been evacuated. A pleasant surprise considering all the disruption that residents had endured, and it was appreciated.

Off we went, back again to the wilds of Baddaginnie, but this time for only one night. Although we had only been back home in Bright for a few days, it really didn't feel like we had left my sister's front driveway.

The Bushfire Advice had once again been downgraded to 'watch and act' so we thought, 'stuff it,' we've had enough of all this and departed first thing the next morning. Having endured bushfires in the past while living in Bright, and they were a lot more dangerous and intent than those we endured in early 2020, we vowed that next time, and if there was a next time, we would simply drive over to Paynesville and sit out any emergency. But, and there is always a but, Paynesville and the East Gippsland area had also been greatly affected by bushfires, so who knows where we will be?

Chapter 17

The long and the short of all this is, life goes on and we did manage the seven-and-a-half-hour trip again via the Hume Highway and the Princes Highway. Paynesville was still in the grip of a post-bushfire depression. The streets were quiet especially when you consider it should have been booming and the main tourism time for the year. The newsagent said they were down over $50,000 in turnover for the first three weeks of January. Although not directly impacted by the fires, people sought the safety of their homes in the major centres of Melbourne. Only time and a concerted media promotion were going to turn around those tourist towns both in the North-East of Victoria and far East Gippsland.

We needed the space and freedom of the Gippsland Lakes as there was only so much of the gloom and doom in the North-East from the fires. When we arrived after our long drive, would you believe it, Bright had just experienced close to seventy-five millimetres of rain as soon as we had left. At least the threat of the bushfires would have subsided both at home and in the East Gippsland region.

We always enter Paynesville via the main road that emerges onto the foreshore in front of the stretch of shops that front the foreshore area. It feels like a coming of home and gives us an immediate view of the lake and over to Raymond Island.

Smoke was still a bit of an issue, but nothing a good westerly or northerly wind wouldn't fix. Being the week before the Australia Day long weekend, there was hope around town that the region might well have a few visitors. This did happen. Whether it was the pressure from the media saying that the bushfire regions were safe or maybe the public's curiosity to see how bad the situation really was.

A breath of fresh air, and still with a week left of the school holidays, tourists made the drive back to the area. The 'watch and act' warning issued had been lifted by the authorities was removed and this seemed to be the catalyst for the change of heart. A generous south-westerly breeze had sprung up and the place regained a sense of purpose.

The thing that really did surprise us was the locals appeared to be relatively content with their situation. Businesses were suffering and that was a worry, but life went on down beside the lake.

Needing to have a look around the area further east, we decided one morning to take the relatively short drive to Lakes Entrance, or as the locals prefer, 'Lakes'. Thinking that we should try and support their tourism and spend a few dollars and while there have, a bit of a fishing session. Surely there would be fish biting somewhere. The plan was to park adjacent to the large footbridge that links the main commercial area to the Ninety Mile Beach.

We had the romantic notion of spending an hour or two on the ocean beach, me fishing while my wife was going to do her best gazing wistfully out to sea between reading her book. As it has been said that sometimes the best-laid plans can come unstuck. I felt like a pack horse loaded up for a discovery trek across Australia. Fishing basket slung across my shoulders, bait box in one hand along with the steel rod holder and my fishing rod. In the other was a folding seat for my better half, all this was topped off with the largest straw hat found on the face of the earth. While my wife had the other essentials necessary for the quiet time on the sand. Stan was on his lead and doing his best to drag my wife across the footbridge.

As we were making our way across several anglers, we can't say, 'fishermen' any more, who were looking quite happy with what they were doing. I couldn't help myself than edge over and try to hear what all the fuss was about. The words, 'king fish are biting' was enough to give even the most useless anglers hope of catching one.

As we were on a mission to the famous 90 Mile Beach, those kingfish would just have to wait. As we neared the other end of the bridge, people were enjoying their time on the small paddle boats off to the left. Immediately in front of us was the beachside café and the rather imposing Lakes Entrance Surf Life Saving Club building. For some obscure reason, I said to my wife, "hang on for a moment, there is a sign with a dog on it." Sure enough, 'no dogs on the beach from November to April.' 'Bugger,' I thought to myself. There was nothing to do but retrace our steps back across the bridge to our car.

Feeling the urgent need to drown my bait, the other option was to make our way back to the area known as Bullock Island. Since our last visit, the local East Gippsland Council had been hard at work improving the area.

For God knows how long, the area seemed to be off the radar as far as tourists were concerned.

The area at the end of the road primarily served the needs of the local fishing industry and shipping that serviced the offshore oil platforms. As far as I can remember, at the end of this short road there has always been the Fisherman's Co-Op where freshly-caught seafood has been available for the public to purchase. Whether it was through rose-coloured glasses, or my memory isn't as good as it should be, I can recall huge quantities of fresh seafood being available behind the glass display windows. On our recent visit, maybe one of those times when once again we didn't catch a solitary fish, we wandered in hoping to find something that appealed to us. Not anymore, it seems that most of the local seafood must be transported directly to the Melbourne wholesale market. There were only a couple of species on offer, maybe only to keep up appearances, but what was there was a little expensive as far as we were concerned. For example, one quite small crayfish, or as some call them, lobsters were available for $135.00. And that was the price per kilogram.

Scuttling out as fast as one of those crabs being taken just around the corner from one of the two jetties on Bullock Island, we too gave up and drove the half an hour back to Paynesville.

Chapter 18

Still, with the fresh prawns still smelling okay, there was only one option left, and that was to drown the remaining bait at the Progress Jetty just down the end of where we stay. This time, I was a lot less loaded up as I only needed the essentials, not the camping exercise that had taken place earlier. Being in the middle of the Australian summer, the temperature was still rather hot, but the ever-present smoke haze seemed to shield the heat a little bit.

As soon as I reached the start of the jetty it was apparent that hordes of others were intent on invading my space. It does sound somewhat pretentious, but that's how it felt. Leisure craft were coming and going continually from both sides of the jetty. Although, according to the sign on the grassed area, the Progress Jetty is the longest of its kind on all the Gippsland Lakes. It would take a crippled duck no more than two minutes to reach the end, so it gives you some idea of the size.

As I reached 'my' spot, there was a bloody yacht moored where I had last been successful catching a few bream, and one solitary mullet. People were coming out of the woodwork; two large cruisers had berthed further along, and their passengers were enjoying the afternoon. Right beside me were three young teenagers swimming around where I had visions of fishing. They then decided to do their utmost to antagonise me by jumping off the jetty on either side of where I was sitting on my cane fishing basket. Oh well, at least the weather was pleasant, and I pretended all this wasn't happening. Several others were making their way along the jetty towards me. I could almost guess what they were going to ask. 'Are they biting?' and 'how many have you caught?' 'Lovely day, I have only been here for a few minutes, but let's hope there is something in the water apart from these little bastards,' well, that's what I felt like saying, but, no, just a polite 'nothing yet, but I am always hopeful.'

After enduring the constant barrage of the teens beside and under me, I was almost on the brink of packing up and conceding defeat. Well, at least the afternoon was warm and pleasant, but then something happened. A slight tug on my line, and then bang! The rod was almost pulled out of my hands with such force that the tip of the rod was hovering above the surface of the water. 'My god, I think I've caught a bloody whale,' I said to myself. I had a quick glance around to see if there was anyone else about to witness my victory.

No such luck, the others all seemed to be too occupied with what they were involved in to worry about me. In an instant, I attempted to pull the rod up from the surface and reduce the drag on the reel to allow the fish or whatever it was not to break the line. No matter how hard I tried, the rod wouldn't budge from its prone position. Just as quickly as the attack on my baited hook had started, the fish made its escape. My eight-pound fishing line was no match for the monster of the deep, and so we parted ways. I think back often about what would have occurred if I had managed to land the fish. Would I have returned it to the water, or kept the beast, to be enjoyed for dinner? I think I would have photographed the culprit and kept the photo record and returned it to its mother. As one of my sons, who is a fishing fanatic once said, 'I'm a lover of fishing, not a killer.'

As I made my way back along the jetty, I thought no one is going to believe my story, no fish (again), and no record of the event. Later that day I wandered into the local news agency to relate my tale. 'I've heard about the huge king fish that have been seen around the jetty, so bad luck, maybe next time,' said the owner. End of story, but there will be another time.

Chapter 19

On our return to Bright, one major achievement had been achieved. The Great Alpine Road had been reopened. We were intrigued to see what all the fuss had been about over the past four weeks with all the fires in the region. As we made our way out of Bairnsdale and headed towards the affected area of Sarsfield, it was staggering to travel past many properties that had been destroyed by the bushfires. It was either through particularly good luck or through diligent fire protection that some properties avoided being burnt. No matter how many times over many years we experience these fires, it still reminds us that we live in one of the most fire-prone areas in the world.

In the most recent fires, which have just passed in early 2020, it was fascinating to see how fast the Australian bush can regenerate. Just north of the small township of Bruthen, a large area was burnt prior to Christmas 2019, and as we were making our first trip back along via the Great Alpine Road since the fires, large areas of the bush had already begun regrowing. Bracken fern was already covering the ground and most of the Australian Eucalypt trees had begun to send out whispery new growth. We can only hope that in another twelve months the only visible reminder would be a few charred tree trunks throughout the landscape.

After having endured endless trials and tribulations of last season's fires, we felt like we needed a break, not only from the constant undertones of 'do we need to evacuate again, surely not?' But the need to find a bit of personal space from the normal humdrum of life in a small town. Fortunately, either we had a bit of foresight, or we were plain lucky, we had booked a cruise for eleven nights from Sydney late the previous year.

Having a now fourteen-month-old King Charles Spaniel named Stan, we were beginning to feel a bit guilty about leaving him in a kennel for the two weeks. Given that he is a fantastic dog, he was really driving us to distraction. The breed is well-known as suffering from separation anxiety and could not bear to be left alone even for short periods.

The thought was that a cruise to somewhere relatively exotic could be the thing we were looking for. Two weeks away from the worries of family, the tourists and the bushfire concerns are what we booked. Stan was booked into the kennels at Chiltern for his first long-time stint in jail, or so it felt to us.

The plan was for an eleven-night cruise with two nights in Sydney prior to departing from Circular Quay in Sydney. It was on a Sunday after our weekly dog lessons at nearby Myrtleford, that after returning to Bright, loading up the car with the suitcases and Stan and retracing our route through Myrtleford, Beechworth and onto Chiltern. We didn't think to mention our plans to Stan as we had no desire to upset him. When you think about it, it was us who began to feel a bit guilty leaving him in the kennels.

Our flight confirmation had been sent to our phone but being over the age of sixty-five this was indeed a novelty. Given the opportunity, both Karen and I would much prefer to have a paper boarding pass in our hands rather than one of those strange digital patterns glaring up at us from our phones.

We finally made our way into the secure parking area of the Albury Airport. We were almost there, it was only the check-in to go, and we could finally think our holiday was about to start. As we made our way towards the check-in counter, it became obvious that we had arrived far too early. "It's better to be too early than too late," I said to my wife, who immediately began to roll her eyes at the thought of having to wait another hour and a half before we even got near the cabin door.

The Albury Airport had recently undergone a major upgrade of all the facilities in the terminal building. It now has all the modern facilities that can be expected in a large regional airport. It certainly had come a long way since our first visit a couple of decades earlier. On our first visit, the luggage was removed from the aircraft and placed onto the top of what appeared to be a dray with wagon wheels attached. If you think this is a bit of an exaggeration, it was then towed into a tin shed by a tractor. Today there are two baggage carousels in the brand-new arrivals area.

The only thing to do was to grab some coffee and just wait. Eventually, the Qantas staff returned to their desks, and we could finally get rid of our suitcases and proceed through security and into the departure lounge. No phone calls from home, "maybe there is something wrong. should I call home and see if everything is fine?" suggested my much-better half. "Let's just pretend our phone is switched off," I sheepishly replied, and so that was the plan.

Our flight number was called, not overly exciting as you would have thought, as there wasn't another flight for another half an hour, but we did feel somewhat excited as we made our way to the scanner and presented our phone to the lady waiting for us. I quickly mentioned to my wife, "I wonder how we would have fared if my phone had run out of power?" "What do you mean, it is fully charged isn't it?" "Just joking," and then her eyes took a sharp glance directly in my direction.

No matter how many times we both make our way onto the tarmac apron and follow the lines to the steps of the aircraft at Albury, or in fact, any other smallish regional airport, it does have the feel of travelling in a bygone era. Most of those large airports that are in most of the capital cities have those large and cavernous airport bridges. Once past the electronic check-in, it's through the tunnel of no return. Follow the person in front and no jokes about terrorists or swine flu, but in more recent times, Coronavirus. But when making your way along the tarmac, it's generally windy, either from the elements or other aircraft in the vicinity there is always the opportunity, to say, 'that's it, I'm not happy,' and feel the need to go home.

Those good people at Albury either knew we were getting a bit older, or it was part of the recent upgrade at the airport, but a wonderful new ramp was waiting for us at the base of the aircraft. No steps, thank God. "Time to switch off the phone," said my wife, "I've done that half an hour ago," so there we were, all alone apart from the other sixty-odd passengers squeezed into the aircraft.

Take offs, according to my wife, are nowhere near as terrifying as landings. I know this, as when we leave the runway, I can still have some feeling in my fingers. When we come into land, it's generally a couple of minutes after the wheels hit the tarmac that some feeling returns to my fingers and hands. I really don't know how this helps relieve the tension, but it does for my wife.

Enough of all this introspection, as soon as the seat belt sign was removed by the captain it was time to sit back and enjoy the flight to Sydney. The wine was offered as was a small box of something salty and nice. We have realised that if the flight attendants are in a good mood, it's a two-glass flight to Sydney, but if they have had a long day, just the single plastic glass will be offered. Cheers, it was a two-glass flight, and the empty ones were gathered on the approach into Sydney.

When the bags were collected from the Sydney Airport baggage area, there was only one more gauntlet to run. That was the dreaded Sydney taxi service. We waited in the line for our grumpy and broody driver to make his way along the rank. Not knowing what to expect, our spirits were immediately dampened as soon as our driver dragged himself out of his vehicle. Was it not a good day, or was he just not in a happy place? Who knows, but having no alternative, we passed him our bags and got in. 'Park Royal Hotel in Darling Harbour please.' Trying to sound as pleasant as possible under the circumstances.

Once the formalities were over and we were on our way, he was driving like a man possessed, "hold on tight," I quietly said to my wife. A mumble came from his clenched teeth, what I quickly worked out was our need to travel through the Sydney toll roads or not? "Whatever suits you so long as we end up at the Park Royal in Darling Harbour, thanks." And so, it was, not another word was spoken, but we did end up at the right hotel and $50.20 poorer.

Not having ever lived in Sydney, and let's face it probably couldn't afford to do so anyway, I still am amazed that anyone can find their way around the maze of inner-Sydney let alone the area we were now staying for two nights. We made our way to the reception and thankfully they had our booking. I always have a bit of a concern when booking online that our name is on their booking register.

We made our way up to the fifth floor and of course, my wife with her uncanny sense of direction got out of the elevator, turned left, while I headed to the right. I really should have just followed her, and all would have been fine. The room was just like any other, but the view this time was different. Darling Harbour was visible through the towers of office blocks, and directly below was a convoluted piece of engineering named, the Western Distributor and the Cross-City Tunnel.

With the lights of Cockle Bay Wharf and the distant restaurant strip beckoning, it was time to make our way out of the safety of our hotel and see what all the fuss was about Darling Harbour. I asked for directions from the reception and was informed, 'go out the front door, turn right and follow the path to the intersection and then take the pedestrian walkway left and you will eventually find your way into Darling Harbour itself.'

Having been a Boy Scout in my youth I knew it was important to follow directions, so it shouldn't be too hard to find our way to our destination. Out we went, turned right and entered what could only be described as a place that would not have been out of place in a horror movie. The dark and enclosed area had obviously been a road in a previous incarnation, as there were directions painted onto the surface, stating, 'no stopping or parking.' This was now what can only be described as a concrete cavern with a large security camera decorating the single light post. Gathered below the now-glowing light was a group of very suspicious-looking people huddled together.

Although seemingly oblivious to the passing crowds of office workers that were walking along the narrow-designated walkway hurrying home or off to end-of-week drinks, those who were huddled together did appear to be watching those who passed. We immediately joined the workers and headed to the intersection of Sussex Street and Druitt Street.

It was not long before the safety and security of The Cockle Bay precinct was reached, even if we did need to stagger down the stairs at the Druitt Street Landing. I don't know about you, but when we reach the age of our 60s the need to start looking for lifts or elevators springs to mind. Steps they were, not too bad walking down, but as the old saying goes, 'what goes down must go up,' well, I think it's the other way around, but in this case, they would need to be tackled later.

We wandered all over the Darling Harbour precinct looking for somewhere to have dinner. It soon became obvious that the need to eat something sooner than later was beginning to be the top of our mission. Looking at the menus outside the various restaurants that were located overlooking the water, one that did appeal was Cyren. The food menu looked appealing and being almost full persuaded us to wait for a table.

An over-zealous waiter escorted us to a table a couple of rows back from the front of the restaurant. We ordered and enjoyed a couple of dishes and a couple of glasses of white wine. One thing that did get our attention, was halfway through our meal, three people sat down in front of us and ordered their meals. Two males and a single female comprised this group.

The young lady seemed to be sitting beside her male friend, while the single male sat on the other side of the table. I have always been amused by what other diners order, especially if we are waiting for our meals to be served to our table. On this occasion, while we were watching the world go by, the diners in front of us had their food delivered. The couple sitting on the left was presented with one of the largest seafood platters I have ever seen. A small lobster was proudly sitting on top of the pile, surrounded by various prawns, fried pieces of fish, a few scallops, several fresh oysters, and the ubiquitous fried chips. I immediately thought that all three of the diners would take a fair bit of time to consume what was in front of them. Both males seemed to be the young fit sporty types, while the young lady did look like she needed a good feed. One of those modern, well-dressed, apart from those torn jeans, that for some reason appear to be fashionable. One who must have every moment of her life accounted for, work, gym, and no eating.

Shortly after the seafood platter had been delivered, and by the way, we did notice the price on the menu, $150.00, and then another dish was presented to the single male. Yes, you guessed it, a medium pizza. I said to my wife, "this'll be interesting, let's see how they go with all that food."

The male who had ordered the platter appeared to be relishing the challenge. While his partner prepared to barrel in so as not to miss out. I was wrong. She took her plate, daintily grabbed her knife and fork and proceeded to prize off the smallest portion of lobster known to man, or in this case, to woman. There was no way either she was going to spill a morsel of lobster sauce on her pristine white shirt or do any damage to her bathroom scales.

Our dinner had arrived, so it was time to eat. Lovely salt and pepper calamari for me and my wife enjoyed her pasta dish. The occasional glance over to our neighbours revealed that the pizza eater was going well while the seafood platter still looked rather the same. She, seemed to be finished while he, began to have that glazed look in his eyes which screamed, 'what to hell have I ordered all this food for?'

We declined the offer of dessert, but instead had another glass of wine. We paid our bill, took one last look at our fellow diners and made our way back out into the throng of fellow tourists.

As we made our way back towards those bloody steps, we mentioned that "it was good to be away, and let's hope the cruise will be as good as we had hoped." Up those steps, and back the way we had come, but when we entered the concrete bunker, the area had a feeling of danger. More undesirables were stationed in the gloom, so this time there was no eye contact, we just headed for the safety of the large rotating glass door and in no time back in our room with its closeted view.

I checked our emails that evening as we did have the next day planned in Sydney, and to our surprise, the following from Royal Caribbean stated, 'due to the recent outbreak of the Coronavirus the New Caledonia Government has closed access to Isle De Pines, Mare and Lifou. Alternative ports will be arranged, if possible.'

Fantastic, great, where were we going to be, who knew? We certainly did not. At the time it really didn't matter as there was the next day to enjoy before we made our way onto the ship. My wife has the desire sometimes to eat out for breakfast. Thinking that breakfast where we were staying did seem far too much to pay, we decided to eat out and not return till the end of our day exploring Tooronga Zoo and its surroundings.

And so, off we went. Back through the concrete cavern, but this being a Monday morning, dozens of commuters were making their way on foot through the area, we did feel a lot safer than the night before. Our target was to end up at Circular Quay and find somewhere for breakfast overlooking the area. This meant us walking down those stairs once again and then turning right and heading for the nearest ferry terminal. Walking straight past the Darling Harbour Wharf for some strange and inexplicable reason, we continued along until we finally found the Barangaroo Wharf Terminal to purchase a daily ticket.

Chapter 20

Being in our mid-60s and coming from rural Victoria, we did not really have a clue about how to purchase a ferry ticket unless it was from Circular Quay. The ticket booth appeared to be the home of moths and spiders so we wandered around trying to find someone who might have something to do with the ferry service. A lady with the logo of Sydney Ferries appeared out of nowhere and told us to 'swipe our credit card under the scanner thing and for $6.50 each that will get you to Circular Quay, and then go to the transport office and buy a day pass.' 'Thanks, we'll do that,' and off she disappeared to where she came from.

The ferry arrived as we were still fumbling with our credit card, so there was just enough time to hurry down to the ferry entrance and jump aboard. There is always something magical about being on one of the ferries and especially when travelling under the Sydney Harbour Bridge. Water was glistening in the morning sunshine; doesn't that sound a bit over the top? But it really did, especially when you consider Sydney had woken up and boats and people were all over the place.

As we made our way under the bridge and turned into Circular Quay, I had this funny feeling we might have got our dates mixed up. But to my relief, it was another cruise ship preparing to load up with another couple of thousand passengers and sail off into the Pacific.

As instructed, we found the Department Transport Office hidden under the overhead railway tracks and waited in the small queue to be attended to. For the grand total of $2.50 per adult, once we provided proof that we were indeed 'Seniors,' we then went to pay with cash. "Sorry, sir, we don't deal in cash here, you'll need to use a credit card." 'Really,' I thought to myself, 'are we really turning into a cashless society?' But, when you consider that for your $2.50 as a senior, you can travel all day on the wonderful Sydney Ferry system, plus bus and trains, it is a remarkable benefit being over the age of sixty in Australia.

The next mission was to find somewhere for breakfast, although time was moving on, we made our way around to the other side of Circular Quay to one of those waterfront cafés that scream, 'look at me, aren't I in a wonderful location.'

We found one that looked right for us, waited to be shown a table and then immediately moved to another. The reason? My wife definitely did not feel like looking at a concrete pillar. Fair enough, I did have the best view of watching the world go by and overlooking the water. Problem solved, just a quick shuffle to another table and all was well.

The young and very indifferent waiter eventually found his way in our direction. God, talk about either being up himself or did he not want to be working in the café, he reluctantly took our order and sidled back from where he had come from. We could only presume that with his heavy European accent he was in Australia on a working holiday. Breakfast of fresh fruit was just what we needed, and a quick coffee and we were out of there as soon as possible.

Back into the crush for the Taronga Zoo ferry, we did not have to wait long before the rest of our day's adventure began. I had only very vague memories of my one and only previous visit to the zoo, as from my calculations it was close to sixty years ago. I recall being pushed around the zoo in a pusher after the short ferry ride across the harbour. Would things have changed in that time? We were about to find out.

According to the lady who greeted all those who made their way to the lower entrance of the zoo after alighting, sounds a bit pretentious, but that is how it was, we were all invited to make our way to the top of the zoo either by the free bus shuttle or via the free cable car. The cable car was far more appealing so off we went. No one told us that there were a substantial series of steps up to the entrance to the cable car building. Eventually, and I do mean eventually, we arrived at the cable car front doors.

Within minutes we arrived at the top station. I can only wonder at the effort that it took for my parents to push me and my brother up all those winding pathways and steps all those years ago. Today the entire area is one of the leading zoos in the world. Overlooking the magnificent Sydney Harbour, it really does Sydney proud.

Tickets purchased, and with the benefit of the Seniors card, only $39.00 per adult. We grabbed a map and set off to explore all that was available. Thankfully, the entire zoo is a walk-down affair. Beginning from the top, the plan was to follow the well-worn path down through the various exhibits and all the animal enclosures. Stop at one of the food outlets then eventually wind our way to the bottom and onto the ferry wharf and back into the city.

We decided that although the Taronga Zoo was a place that would appeal to international tourists, to us it really felt more like a large amusement park with the collection of animals tossed in from time to time. There was even a thousand-seat outdoor seating area for the daily seal 'show.' As far as we were concerned, the Australian native animals were ho-hum, there are more kangaroos, wallabies, lizards, and snakes within a kilometre of home in Bright. Even platypuses are found in our local creeks and rivers only a noticeably short walk from home. Koalas are abundant in the Australian bush and bloody possums are the bane of life at home.

"Enough of this, shall we make our way back to Darling Harbour, or would like to walk back up the hill and go around again?" I asked my wife. There was a quick rolling of the eyes as we made our way back along the Athol Wharf Road to the ferry, which by complete chance was waiting to depart.

Back in Circular Quay, where to go next? Thinking it was time for a quiet drink overlooking the harbour, I suggested we jump on the ferry to Rose Bay where I believed there were a couple of places open to the public on the water's edge. It was not long before the Rose Bay Wharf came into view. We jumped off and headed left for what looked like a promising place for a quiet one or two.

Although the Catalina Restaurant did look fantastic, it did not seem the place for us as it appeared to be exceptionally fine dining, and with a price to suit its location. On the sign at the front entrance, lunch could be ours for $165.00 per person, it was a bit difficult to comprehend that much for lunch after our $20.00-for-two lunch at the zoo. A little further along the path was a lovely-looking bar which could have suited us, but of course, that was closed till later.

There was nothing much else to do but return to the wharf and wait for the next ferry to take us back to Circular Quay. In a little over half an hour, the same ferry returned to ferry us back, but the bonus was that it was travelling all the way back to Darling Harbour.

Back in Darling Harbour, there was either the walk back up those bloody stairs or a short diversion first to find that elusive bar that was missing earlier. The Waterfront Bar screamed at us, 'come on in, we're open.'

By either good luck or good management, we were seated right at the front facing the reasonably large Ferris wheel. Popular with dozens of visitors, it was delightful watching the smiling faces and antics of those riding around in circles. A couple of glasses of white wine and we were ready to join those who were happily seeing Darling Harbour in all its glory. Dusk was settling over the area, and it did seem like we had been transported back in time to our childhood. No problems and not a care in the world. Was all this romantic stuff about to change, of course, it would, we were boarding the Voyager of the Seas first thing in the morning.

After a slight dose of nostalgia, it was back around the steps, through the concrete cavern and into the Park Royal Hotel. Dinner was a couple of smallish meals from the bar, and in bed asleep by nine p.m. "God, we must be getting old," I said to my wife.

The next morning, we gave in to the price for breakfast at the hotel, packed up and left by ten-thirty a.m. A short taxi ride to Circular Quay and we were there. It was huge, the Voyager of The Seas, and from a bit of research, when launched in 1990, was the biggest passenger ship in the world. Four thousand passengers plus a crew of close to one thousand seven hundred certainly did get our attention.

We, of course, were early, so Karen made herself at home in one of the waiting lounges while I went on a mission to purchase two bottles of wine for our cabin. Two bottles per stateroom were what was allowed. So off I went on a wine mission. The directions were, back up to the police station, turn left and it is almost opposite. "Great," I said to my wife, "I won't be long."

Half an hour later, not a bottle shop was sighted, I was about to give up when an old hotel came into view. 'That'll do,' I thought to myself. So, in I went to the bar and purchased two of the cheapest bottles of red wine they had. I know that sounds a little bit of a cheapskate but at $30.00 per bottle that was indeed enough.

Back to the cruise ship terminal in a little under forty-five minutes. "What took you so long? I thought I might be going on this cruise by myself," said my wife. We made our way to the check-in as directed and were surprised to be ushered through past all the other passengers waiting in one of those convoluted passenger lines that you find in airport check-in areas. Apparently as we had booked a suite that gave us that privilege.

Before long, we were making our way along the walkway and onto the ship. We knew where we were going, and it was not long before we were walking into our stateroom number 6694. All the bells and whistles, separate lounge area and bed big enough for three. The bathroom did have a feeling of being locked in the early 1990s and really, could have done with a bit of renovation.

Feeling the need for something to eat, we made our way up to the Windjammer Buffet. I have a complete dislike for the buffets on ships, while the food is always good, the constant need to find a place to sit is way beyond my level of patience.

Enough said about the buffet, all passengers were expected to make their way to their designated Muster Station as shown on their cruise cards. Four p.m. was the time and half an hour later it was time to set sail off into the blue Pacific. We all did as we were directed, watched as the safety drill was explained and then dispersed somewhere to watch the departure.

By six p.m. we were still sitting at the cruise terminal having not moved an inch. The word soon spread, that one of those small yellow boats that ferry the crew ashore when a new port is reached, had fallen off the side of the ship and into the water facing the Sydney Opera House. Not a word was said over the public address system, but a couple of the passengers did video the event with their phones. Was this a bit of an omen? Possibly, but we will have to wait and see.

Cruise ship passengers can be a funny lot, some, like us, just go about their business without much fuss while others, let the world know that 'we are Diamond Club members,' and for those who seem to spend their entire lives on one of the Royal Caribbean ships, they can reach the lofty height of 'Diamond Plus.' The first category I believe is achieved once a passenger has spent more than eighty days at sea on one of their ships. God only knows what is required for the Diamond Plus, but it will not concern us in the near or distant future.

Putting all that aside, our first night in the Grand Dining Room was not as we had expected. It usually goes without saying that the dining room on most passenger ships maintains a certain degree of a dress standard. We have always thought dining in one of those grand rooms has been a bit special and always a privilege. On our first night, in this case, other guests thought it quite the thing to roll up dressed in tee shirts and shorts. Not to be thought of as a snob, but I did feel like standing up and saying, 'hey, you lot, go up to the buffet if you can't dress a little better.'

That evening we made our way to the Royal Theatre for the first of many evening shows. How can I put this? Really ordinary, apparently the magician who was trying to impress the crowd had appeared on one of the major American television shows. Were we supposed to be impressed? Who knows, but what was dished up to those there on that night did leave us with the thought it must not take much to amuse their audiences.

The next morning, we made our way to the main dining room and joined the vast throng of passengers waiting to be shown to a table. Breakfast on this cruise was either up in the Windjammer Buffet where we were sure the scene was still one of chaos, or in the main dining room. We chose the dining room as things in the past have always been far more civilised. You wait at the door and are then escorted to either a table for two or "would you like to share?" Having experienced both in the past, we just go with the flow. On this occasion, we were escorted by a waiter who was well-versed in the procedure. Right hand stuck up like a periscope in a submarine. "Quick, follow that arm," I muttered to my better half.

For some inexplicable reason, the tables we were directed to in the mornings were as far away as possible, this really wasn't an issue, as on the Voyager of The Seas, breakfast was a bloody help-yourself-buffet. At least the surroundings were pleasant, and most passengers did observe some form of patience. We sat as directed, placed our cruise card on the table and immediately made our way over to select our breakfast.

It was always interesting, as most of our fellow passengers seemed to be of similar age as us. Of course, there were a few exceptions, but generally that was the case. Conversations quickly took place, and from our experience, most people were engaged in topics such as 'oh, how much was your travel insurance?' and 'how much do you pay for your health cover and who do you deal with?'

The rest of the day was spent avoiding the crowds, especially the starboard side of the ship. Up on the pool deck and on the promenade deck, where smoking is permitted. It was like fighting your way through the smoke in a bushfire in both places. On Australian ships that we have travelled on previously, smokers were actively discouraged and were sent to either the rear or stern, hidden away corners, usually one of the windiest locations and out of sight. But the Voyager of The Seas being an American ship does not follow Australia's strict non-smoking guidelines.

Our place of solitude, well, with at least forty others doing the same thing, was up on deck fourteen overlooking the swimming pool area. The Pool Bar and Lounge was one of the only places on the ship where a passenger could look out and gaze at the ocean on both sides of the ship. Perched high above the hundreds of bathers milling around the two swimming pools and four large spa pools.

The first couple of days out of Sydney, the weather was beginning to feel a little warmer, and the migration out to the large pool area had begun in earnest. Hundreds of passengers, mostly middle-aged and older grabbed every available sun-lounger and claimed it as their own territory. The process was a bit like claiming Australia for King and Country. As soon as the 'blue towel' was placed, it was yours.

Back to the Pool Bar and Lounge up on level fourteen, it was fascinating to watch the antics and goings on down on the pool deck. Many of those males in the older bracket appeared to have the stature and colouring of old Queensland cane toads. Big, bloated, and brown. The overall effect was completed with a large gold chain, and if we were unlucky, speedos, or as they are sometimes known in Australia, Budgie Smugglers. While the women of the same age did present a little better, their hair was always blond, and a glass of wine always in hand. Children were there but in much smaller numbers, but those who inhabited the pool area seemed to be unsupervised. Running riot like there was no tomorrow, occupying the spas, pools and generally being annoying to all. I felt like going down there from our lofty height and asking, 'shouldn't you lot be home and going to school?'

The day did progress and, secreted away up in the lofty heights of deck fourteen, we continued to enjoy the benefits of being cocooned away from the others. The night had been scheduled as being a Formal Night. Captain Wu, who was Chinese, and the rest of the senior officers were scheduled to make one of their rare appearances in front of the passengers.

So, anticipating one of these evenings, we dressed accordingly. Me, suit and tie, and my wife, all in black with a couple of accessories. As we made our way down one flight of stairs to the central atrium area, we found ourselves amid one of those shopping frenzies, that can only be found on cruise ships. Dozens of shoppers were frantically seeking through a mountain of 'discounted handbags and jewellery.' Some of our fellow passengers were dressed a bit more formally than the throng, but only a few.

We decided to take the opportunity to enjoy a glass of wine in the Irish Pub. Feeling somewhat conspicuous, we lingered for a short time then made our way further along the Royal Parade, as it is called. One of the benefits of the formal night was that the Voyager of The Seas offered a free glass of sparkling wine to be addressed by the captain and his senior officers. With a great deal of fanfare, Captain Wu was asked to make his way across the walkway above the Royal Promenade. We, of course, listened to his wise and important words if our glass was full and then joined in the applause for him and his senior officers. All the while the frantic shoppers were still burrowing away on the tables looking for their bargains.

We were fortunate to have booked a mini suite which apparently gave us the benefit of not having to queue up for entrance to dinner in the Grand Dining Room. We did feel a bit self-conscious about this, but it did not take us too long to get over that.

There must have been a directive from management regarding the seating arrangements in the evenings. On the two formal nights, we appeared to be seated with other dinners who were dressed in a similar fashion. All genuinely nice, but never in the same seats or area. One family group of five adults and one child were always seated together and always at the same table. Did they have a booking, who knew? Maybe they were part of the earlier prescribed set of dining, but I had my doubts. They wandered in seemingly whenever they chose, and their table was there waiting for them. Noticing that they were always dressed in black whether it be black tee shirts, shorts, and those 'active wear' leggings for the women, it did appear to be a bit odd. All five of the adults struggled to wear all the gold and silver chains around their necks, but the overall appearance was finished off with an abundance of tattoos. The men all sprouted greying ponytails while the women all maintained the same black hair colour.

After dinner was over, the announcements came over the public address system explaining that due to three of the crew showing mild signs of being unwell, they had been isolated somewhere down the bottom of the ship. I think it must have been one of those places passengers are never shown, but the outcome was that we were still stopping at Noumea as scheduled. But there would be further announcements the following day.

We carried on, as usual, dining with our new best friends, most of whom we would never see again, especially when there were over three and a half thousand other passengers. It was a little odd with half the diners dressed for something special, while the others appeared as if they had just rolled in from the mad shopping frenzy a couple of decks above.

After dinner, off we went to the Royal Theatre and waited to be entertained. I know that sounds a bit pretentious but there was only so much 'entertainment' we could cope with in one twenty-four-hour period. As a treat we were told, one of Australia's top international entertainers was going to perform for us. I wondered who he was and did not have to wait too long before his image and name were up in lights on large screens on either side of the stage.

Our ever-enthusiastic 'Cruise Director' skipped onto the stage and introduced him, and to save any repercussions, let's call him, 'Bob Smith.' 'Bob' bounded out of the shadows and into the spotlights. He belted out a couple of fine songs, and they were pleasing to the ear, but then proceeded to give us his life story. How he had been on a couple of high-profile American television shows, and in the recent past, had been one of the main actors on an Australian children's television program. Given that from our experience, these cruise ship entertainers are usually on stage twice in one night and for a forty-five-minute stint and that was about it. Half of 'Bob's' time was spent telling us about his background. Well, at least his teeth appeared to be unnaturally white for a person of his age, but I suppose that goes with the job. Being seated at the rear of the lower section of the theatre allowed us to escape under the cover of darkness just moments before the curtain came down, or in this case, the lights came back on.

The next day seemed like the others, breakfast, up to the fourteenth deck, grab a couple of comfortable seats in front of the massive windows overlooking the pool area and watch the activity far below. I have found that in the past, no matter how early you manage to arrive at the desired place, there are always others there before you. Arranged immediately behind the window 'premium tables and seats' are another row of similar seats. Not as good but still worth grabbing. It was in the second row we were relegated to.

Trying not to seem eager, we kept a close eye on all those in front who appeared to be making the slightest movement. Whether it be a simple rearranging of their chair, to placing their book on the table. The anticipation was palpable. "Are they going?" I whispered to my wife. In an instant, "let us go, I think they're off." And with that, there was no way going back, as soon as their bums were off the seats, we had taken their place, and even the seats were still warm.

"Now, whatever we do, like go to the toilet or anything else, one of us has to remain here, okay?" I said quietly to my wife. As we all know, bums keep seats. Fantastic, we could now see down in front and both sides of the ship and, if we stood up, way out in front into the blue Pacific.

One of those things I have, or it could be you especially if you are a male, is a fascination with the weather. Sitting up in the eagle's nest on deck fourteen was a weather watcher's paradise. On this morning, dozens were already out on the sun loungers, wallowing in the two pools, and bouncing around in the four spa pools. In today's climate of pool safety and accountability, there were three lifesavers, or as it said on their uniforms, lifeguards.

Talk about being committed. All three stood there on the side of the pools and spas, looking intently at the water. Were they mesmerised, or was it what was required? Dressed in red shorts, red shirt, red and white cap, they stood either in the water with their white rubber wading sandals on, or on the edges of the pools. Constantly clutching one of those red and white flotation devices. Imagine a slightly curved massive hot dog with a cord attached and that was their mission.

The reason I mentioned the weather was we could see what was heading our way, from up in the 'eagle's nest.' A storm was heading our way, although it was difficult to gauge how far away, but it was heading our way. All those down on the pool deck were oblivious and kept on partying, as the bars had now opened for the day. Regulars could be seen propping up the bar in their normal positions.

It was about to be interesting. As soon as the storm arrived, the scene evolving below was like those red crabs on Christmas Island that you see on television occasionally. Bodies moving as one to the shelter of the side area. The lifeguards were obviously under instructions that, 'under no circumstances were they allowed to shelter out of the rain.'

There was something quite surreal about the lifesavers. All standing at their posts, looking down at the water that was now sloshing all over the edges of the pools. Not a swimmer in sight, let alone in the water. But there was a bonus, one of the off-duty lifeguards made his way over and proceeded to hand over to each of the others, a yellow plastic poncho. At first glance, you could have been mistaken for thinking there were three large yellow condoms standing in the water holding a large red curved hot dog.

And so, the rain continued, but to use a bit of a cliché, 'there was light at the end of the tunnel' or in this case, the rain seemed to be abating. The smoke from the smoking area on the starboard side adjacent to the pool area was beginning to thin as the wind had now increased its speed. I could only presume that it was exciting via the doors and into the Windjammer Buffet. Sure enough, when it was time for a coffee, I alone made my way downstairs to the buffet and noticed the smell. I really don't know what the attraction is to smoking, but it's the freedom of choice we appreciate in Australia, but really beside the pool and adjacent to the buffet. I just do not get it.

As you may have guessed, the weather did clear, and the activities resumed in earnest on the pool deck. No sooner had the rain ceased than several of the crew were out in action. Large rubber squeegees were squeezing every wet and flat surface in the area. I don't suppose there could be anyone slipping over due to the rain. But really, the area had previously been awash with the water both from children, adults, and the movement from the ship in the storm.

People are funny things, especially when you see several continuing to run laps in the rain around the running track. The previous afternoon I felt the urge, it must have been an urge as it is not something I usually can be found doing. Was it the amount of food we had been consuming over the first few days of the cruise or was it the need to find out what all the fuss is about? At home in Bright my usual exercise regime amounts to wandering around our local golf course two or three times a week. Every other day I can usually be seen taking Stan our dog for a walk. On this occasion, the need to 'do a few laps' came out of nowhere. I said to my wife, "I won't be long, I feel the need to go for a walk." "Ok, don't get lost, I'll still be here when you return." Off I went, raced down the two flights of stairs, well, I was in training, of course, and made my way out to the great outdoors.

The pool deck and Windjammer are both on deck eleven. The mysterious running track was located on deck twelve. Mysterious, I hear you ask? Well, for all intentions it was the only place on the ship that could host a running track. The Promenade deck on other fine vessels we have been on is usually the place where those who wish to shed a couple of kilograms can do a few laps. On the Voyager of The Seas, the Promenade deck came to a screeching halt where the Star Lounge protrudes out. So, the only place for those who find the need, or the urge, is deck twelve.

Access is out through a double set of glass doors. The first set must act as a bit of a windbreak or airlock, while the second door is sheltered behind a curved glass screen structure. The weather seemed now bright and sunny, but what I did not realise at the time prior to leaving the inside of the ship, was how bloody windy it was. The wind was so strong as I ventured outside the safety of the clear, curved screen. To use a well-known Australian term, 'the wind was so strong, it would suck the fart out of a camel.'

Around I went, and to be truthful, it was so strong it almost blew me backwards into the side of the ship. 'This is going to be a bit more of a chore than I first thought,' I said to myself. Young women in running gear, old ladies with walkers and super-fit young males were all competing for my small stretch of track. Although the track did have a nice white line painted down the centre, there didn't seem to be any etiquette to the direction in which one was to run, jog, or take the walker for a walk. I just chose the left and departed to the right. All those now back sitting in the sun, down on the pool deck were oblivious to the gale force wind that now was buffeting us true athletes.

I found my slot in the traffic and headed anti-clockwise. Against the wind, I could feel myself being blown backwards, and during one of the bigger gusts, almost fell over in my attempts to push forward. Thinking my wife was watching my progress, I tried hard to remain upright. Powering along at a snail's pace, even the elderly lady with a walker was gaining on me.

A short way around from my starting point, I came across this what appeared to be hidden area of the ship. Not visible from our perch up on the fourteenth deck, the Solarium bar and pool is an adult only area. Out of sight and, more importantly, out of the wind. As I gazed down at the pool and its two spa pools, the scene reminded me of a Queensland municipal swimming pool filled with bloated cane toads. Mostly overweight older males with the sprinkling of their partners trying to stay away from the sun. As we all know in Australia, our sun does terrible things to a person's skin, but from my quick, short glance over the railing, I thought, 'why do they bother?' The damage had been done, so enjoy being away from your demands back at home.

I continued back on my journey around the Solarium Bar and headed back to my starting point. One major difference on the port side, doesn't that sound nautical? Was that the gale-force wind was now propelling me at such speed that I hoped my wife was at least glancing in my direction. I almost broke into a canter but managed to control my pace. Several more laps were completed before I thought, 'what on earth am I doing? All this walking and not chasing a golf ball was becoming a waste of my time.' I made my way back to the stairs, do I walk up the two flights to the sanctuary of my wife, or do I take the lift? At that moment, I heard the unmistakable 'ding' of the lift. I quickly glanced over, and the indicator was pointing up. Did I do the right thing and scale the two flights of stairs? Of course not, I raced over to the lift and got in.

As I left the lift, a quick push with my hands through my now-dishevelled wind-blown hair and I casually strolled across to where my wife was still deeply engrossed in her book. "Did you have a nice walk, dear?" "Didn't you see me fighting the gale force winds so that I will be in great shape for Noumea tomorrow?" "No, sorry, I was too engrossed in my book to even know that you weren't here." Well, at least I was impressed.

That evening we made our way again to the Grand Dining Room and pondered what would be on the menu of fine food and who would our fellow passengers be. We were not disappointed. Food always seemed to be of a particularly good standard if you chose well. While on the other hand, our fellow diners certainly were a diverse bunch. The main topics for the evening were, 'Oh, we've just recovering from our skin cancer operations' and 'we've been on every ship in the world.' I gave my wife a quick glance and muttered under my breath, "you've got to be joking." Another couple our age sitting on one side of us were gladly telling anyone who would listen how many cruises they had been on and when this cruise was over, how they were travelling back to Coogee by train. Doing the washing and getting back on the Voyager of The Seas and repeating the same cruise again. I will tell you something remarkably interesting about all this when we return home.

<h1 style="text-align: center;">Chapter 21</h1>

Early the next morning from our stateroom at the rear of the ship, I could not contain myself. I have always loved arriving early at one of the Pacific's ports. In our past two visits to Noumea, our ships have arrived at the main cruise ship port. Almost smack in the middle of the town, so close that it is only a short stroll into the market and the city. The sights and sounds are so foreign to us in our little pocket of rural bliss in Bright. But there is always a but, on this occasion the Voyager of The Seas was being moored at the city's maritime container wharf. There was nothing remotely tropical and French about disembarking into the midst of a container wharf. Well, there were a few French signs about but apart from that, we could have pulled up at Geelong or Fremantle.

On this trip we broke with our usual practice of getting off at the port and finding our own way around the town, by pre-booking one of the shore excursions. In this case, we had decided to spoil ourselves and travel out to Iles des canards. Better known to foreign tourists as, Duck Island.

Our free bus shuttle service dropped us along the Rue Jules Ferry at the Cruise Ship Terminal building. The two very delightful, and I should say here, stunning young local tour guides did their best to tell all who were listening about the ins and outs of the free bus service back to the ship. I was sure most of the women were listening, but the men, possibly just dreaming of those two stunning young local women. Dressed in tight tee shirts and noticeably short denim shorts, they presented an exceptionally fine example of local ladies with not a care in the world.

We made our way, dutifully following our guides and were then deposited into the hands of Captain Max. Max and his twelve-seater Zodiac were our form of transport to Duck Island. A quick safety run down from our new best friend, Max. To me and my fellow males on the boat, Max was one of those people who exuded French charm. A total package, or so my wife thought. Max gave us a short spiel about his life and times. It seemed that he spent most of his life sailing his large yacht around the Pacific Ocean. He had recently settled in Noumea and pointed out the small bay where his yacht was permanently moored. Let us put this in perspective. Max, I could guess was in his early 40s, tall, tanned and slightly scruffy. Longish hair blowing slightly in the tropical breeze, the hint of a beard, sun-tanned and extremely confident in his part of the world. I really think that, given the opportunity, all the females would have abandoned ship with Captain Max at the first opportunity.

We males hunkered down for the trip out to the island. Duck Island is tiny. Hardly even room for a pony and a pool. It was explained that all those who were on the trip had reserved sun loungers and were to make themselves at home and Captain Max would be returning in two hours exactly for the return trip to the city. Loungers located, towels and bags placed to secure our seats from the late interlopers who were arriving constantly by ferries.

There we sat, under our separate red umbrellas, watching a most beautiful part of the world go by. It is an interesting place, the island. Tiny, I thought a short walk around would be nice, I was back in under five minutes. A large restaurant area set under the trees, with two high-set long-drop toilets, and a wonderful, large cool bar set below a timber roof, completed the infrastructure. There must have been close to a hundred sun loungers scattered around three sides of the island. Of course, there was a small stall set up near the beach for those wishing to hire snorkelling equipment and sun loungers. I wandered over to see if it was possible to purchase some water, I felt like I must have become invisible.

The two 'beach boys,' not my term, but the lovely French lady behind the bar called them that, so I made my way back the fifty metres or so and asked for the next best thing. One small can of la Biere de Nouvelle-Calédonie Number 1 beer. And a bottle of water. Not too bad a price I suppose the equivalent of $18.00 Australian. I hear you ask; how did I know this was the price in Australian dollars? That's what the delightful French lady took out of my hands. I think I might have been taken for a ride, but who cares? I still have the image lingering on my phone, just to remind me in the future to carry some of the local currency.

It was one of those truly delightful short spans of time on the island and we were a little reluctant to get back onto Captain Max's zodiac, but if global warming does eventuate, I know for sure that Duck Island would be completely submerged as the whole thing wouldn't be higher than two metres above sea level.

After the transfer back to the cruise ship terminal, we felt obligated to make our way into the building. A strong smell of stale urine permeated throughout the central garden area. As we wandered around to the stairs to make our ascent up to the market on the first floor, I said to my wife, "Hey, have a look over there through that open door." "Are they serious? I can see straight into the men's toilet and there's only a short louvre door separating the man from the public while he does his business." She was a little shocked, but I casually said, "that's the French for you, they don't appear to be modest at all."

We made our way up the stairs, and I was sure that, although it had been a few years since our last visit, the same stall holders were still trying to sell the same souvenirs as before. Back down again and where we joined the throng in the blazing sun for the shuttle back to the ship.

Once back on board, we were now too late for lunch in the dining room, so had to endure the buffet. One thing we have found with all buffet-style meals on all the ships we have been on, is to quote Forrest Gump, 'Life's like a box of chocolates, you just don't know what you're going to get.' If ever there was a truer statement, I will eat one of my golf gloves. Because at any one time, there will be one thousand five hundred passengers trying to find somewhere to sit when there are only one thousand seats. I really picked those numbers out of the air, but I am sure you understand what I am saying.

We found two spare and lonely seats at a table that already had three other passengers sitting there. They looked like they had taken up residency for the afternoon, as we all know, it is bums that keep seats. At this time in the afternoon, we were becoming desperate; one, to find somewhere to sit and, second, it was getting close to two o'clock. I sidled over and asked, "excuse me, are those seats taken?" "No, feel free, you are most welcome," came the reply.

"Thanks, I'll just go over and let my wife know." "Come this way, I cannot find another two seats anywhere, they seem fine, just smile and nod and eat as fast as possible." The plan was always the same in the buffet. One of us always sat and reserved the two seats while the other went in search of food. A bit like a hunter and gatherer or so it seemed. Lunch, was it either extremely late or was it an early dinner? Anyhow as soon as it was possible, we scurried out and tackled the three flights of stairs to the safety and sanctuary of the Viking Crown Lounge.

Fortunately, there were a couple of the prime seats and a table overlooking the pool deck. Things had not really changed much since our last visit. Young males were still strutting all over the place like peacocks, always bare-chested and, if possible, holding their stomachs in and flexing their muscles. The young ladies, well, what can I say? It was a 'look at me, aren't I gorgeous?' sort of parade. Wandering, or should I say again, strutting all over the place. Lots of hair flinging as they passed their admiring audience.

One incredible thing that did catch my attention was an older woman. A Muslim, as she was covered from head-to-toe and nowhere as svelte as those young ladies around her. But to her immense credit, she casually strolled up and stepped into one of the spa pools. Fully dressed, and without a care in the world. She was soon joined by a couple of large males, all hairy, big, and adorned with large gold chains. I can only presume they were part of her extended family. It was lovely to see.

After dinner, the announcement was made over the public address system, "Good evening, this is Captain Wu, we have been denied access to our next five ports, so we have secured another three ports to visit. The first will be Tauranga, then The Bay of Islands in New Zealand and then off to Eden on the south coast of New South Wales, we are sorry for the inconvenience. I hope to see you around the ship." And with that, we were headed to the Land of the Long White Cloud, New Zealand.

"Did I really hear that we were now going to Eden in New South Wales?" I asked my wife incredulously. "Yes, dear, that'll be interesting." By complete chance, the lovely couple our age that we were sitting next to at dinner were from New Zealand. Barry and Judith Delahanty. "I bet you weren't expecting that, Barry?" I asked after the announcement was made. "No, we certainly didn't think that was part of the plan, we had been looking to see those islands that we had heard so much about," said Barry. "As a matter where are you both from?" I enquired. "Funny you should mention that, as we live in Tauranga, our next port of call." "What are you going to do, are you both going to get off and go home?" I asked. "We were thinking of getting off, going home for a while and I'll mow the lawns," he said with one of those wry smiles. "We won't tell our family as they'll be all over us like a rash, we'll just keep a low profile and continue the cruise back to Sydney then fly back home, it's our first ever cruise, so we're going to sit back and enjoy the experience."

There was another couple of days cruising back to Tauranga, so the next two days became a bit of a blur. More sitting and watching, but with the bonus of an excursion down to the Star Lounge. We must have been really bored at the time, but we made our way to the front of the Lounge and purchased a book of Bingo tickets. Our other experiences with playing bingo on cruises have been a nice way to pass an hour or so, there was always the chance of winning something. Previously tickets on other ships were $20.00 for ten games, and that was in Australian dollars. In this latest cruise, tickets were $34.00 American, for only four games. I think when the calculations were made, we paid close to $50.00 Australian for four measly bloody games. We did not win a thing, but at least we had a go. Did we attend another bingo session on the ship? Of course not.

After all that excitement, it was time to retreat to the safety and sanctuary of deck fourteen. Two ladies were in residence up on deck fourteen, and they proudly told everyone they were from the Central Coast of New South Wales. Were we supposed to be impressed, who knows? The other lady was named Narelle; poor Narelle could not get a word in. The main and loudest, let's call her Judy, was telling everyone who couldn't help but hear that she was a Diamond Plus passenger with 'her' Royal Caribbean. "Oh, the benefits, free drinks in 'our' lounge from four to six p.m. and free nibbles, oh, I feel so lucky," she told the world. 'As if anyone really cared.' I said to myself, I suppose if that is your life and you have spent tens of thousands of American dollars pursuing this, well so be it.

Chapter 22

After listening to all this rubbish, we could not take any more, so I suggested to my wife, "how about a short walk outside? The fresh air will be good, rather than all the stale stuff up here." A good idea you would have thought. Down we went to the twelfth deck and out into the breeze. More like the gale with which I had previously battled. "I know somewhere out of the wind, follow me." Karen had not had the joy of walking around the pool deck on deck eleven. Was she going to be pleased? I suspected not. Adults and children all congregating on the starboard side out of the wind, but it was like walking into an Australian bushfire. The smoke was so thick it could not have been healthy for all those children there eating plate-loads of hot chips. One of the benefits of the pool deck for those who resided there was the close access to the Windjammer Buffet.

Our exit did not take long, out one door and into another to the sanctuary of the lower decks. Sitting in the R Bar a lady of some age, I really could not work it out nor could my wife, I am thinking maybe mid-seventies sat down beside us. A vision in pink and purple. Long, fine pink hair tied up with an assortment of purple and pink chiffon scarves. Her face was so tight for a person of her age, it didn't look natural. More like a young woman in her late thirties. Polished like a billiard ball. Her clothing was extravagant as was the loudness of her voice. Her fingernails were resplendent, long manicured and painted with colours of the rainbow. "Oh, I don't know how I'm going to cope for the rest of this cruise, I miss my personal beautician so much, I go and see her twice a week."

I quietly said to my wife, "I bet the beautician has large glass doors as this vision in purple and pink must have a lot of money and can see her coming.". She then proceeded to tell anyone who cared all about her troubles and her life. I felt like saying, 'with all this, why didn't you just stay at home and annoy your beautician and not us?'

We needed another place to hide, so made our way back to the sanctuary of our stateroom. We ordered room service; a cheese platter, and a bottle of wine. We sat out on the balcony overlooking the large blue deck and gazed out at the Pacific Ocean trailing off into the distance. Bliss.

I can appreciate the joy and excitement of sailors who venture out into the oceans of the world. Both my wife and I are on the constant lookout for anything of interest that might be 'out there' but, apart from the single occasion off Tahiti when our ship passed the Paul Gaugin vessel, there has not been a thing. How those sailors can handle the oceans and the weather I'll never know, let alone need to find out.

We made our way in the late afternoon back up to deck fourteen and into the Viking Crown Lounge. This time we had been relegated back to the second row. It really did not matter as the dance classes were about to begin. Yes, I hear you say, dance classes. Ballet, old time Pride of Erin or the Cha Cha? No, it was bloody line dancing. Our dancing instructor, well not ours as we were firmly planted on our seats, waltzed in, dressed in his very tight tights, cropped, tight dancer's white shirt and, as my wife would say, 'with an accent to die for.' His hair neatly piled high on his head; he was ready for action.

We had previously witnessed his prowess when leading a dozen or so passengers with his half hour ballet lessons in the same area. This was a totally different thing both in style and his pupils. They were packed in like sardines. Passengers who had obviously never been to the Royal Crown Lounge before. "Oh, we haven't been here before, isn't this fantastic?" they said in their own local dialect. I thought, 'well, there goes the neighbourhood, the place will never be the same again.' And it wasn't. Gone were those quiet and reflective times up on deck fourteen.

"Ok, let us start with the basics, just follow my lead and we'll all have a fantastic time." And follow him they did. Like sheep being chased by a highly trained border collie. He did, and they watched then did the same. I should admit here that if there was another option rather than witness fifty or sixty various shapes and sizes try to line dance I would have been there in a flash. The thing was the entire half hour was absolutely wonderful to witness. So many different ages, sizes and abilities trying to move as one to one of the classics by Billy Ray Cyrus, 'My Achy Breaky Heart.' All led with a smile by our wonderful and lovely, let's call him José, completed another afternoon on the Voyager of The Seas.

That evening after dinner we felt an obligation to make our way again to the Royal Theatre. This evening was showcasing a hypnotist. As far as this form of entertainment goes, I am very cynical.

Chapter 23

By a strange quirk of fate, my late father, Albert (Bert) Badrock, was in his early years a performing hypnotist and went under the stage name of 'The Amazing Mr Alber.' I have only one very vague memory as a very young child being taken to one of my parent's shows somewhere near Williamstown, a few kilometres south-west of Melbourne. After he died a couple of years ago, I was having a bit of a look through his personal papers. I had seen his image of his performing times many years earlier. I was delighted to come across the picture in his papers. It shows a serious-looking young man about the age of twenty-two or three.

As I am writing this, it prompted me to further investigate, The Amazing Mr Alber and his exploits. I find it fascinating that after fifty-seven years he still treasured his days in the spotlight. He had always, for as long as I can recall, liked being in the spotlight. As an amateur hypnotist and later as a magician he loved performing to a crowd.

In his very early times as the 'Amazing Mr. Alber,' both he and my mother travelled throughout Melbourne and the Victorian countryside putting on various shows. The recent papers I have found included such gems as the following from 8th of August 1951.

'*Presenting in the Warrnambool Town Hall.*

On Saturday 8th of September at 8.00 p.m. sharp.

Melbourne's Sensational *Hypnotist* The Amazing Mr. Alber.

A guaranteed Laugh-A-Minute Show.

Bookings open Vin Mills Friday 31.8.1951

In aid of South Warrnambool Kindergarten

Admission 3/6 Children 2/-'

Reading through his memories about these shows, the majority were performed for local charities, and he was one of the best self-promoters I have come across. This leads me to one of those articles that he kept for all those decades. Back in 1951, way before I was born, and a few years prior to television becoming available in Australia, radio was king. Radio station

3AW in Melbourne was one of the popular radio stations operating at the time. 3AW still dominates the commercial radio scene in Melbourne today.

On the eighteenth of August 1951 on the prime listening time of seven thirty p.m. there was a half-hour program called, the Koolmint Show. I can only presume that the half-hour slot was sponsored by the manufacturers of Koolmints. Doug Elliot, the host for the evening program was to give the listening audience a special treat. And I will present the radio interview from the hand-typed couple of pages. A few pieces I will have to improvise as it seems that over all these years, silverfish have chewed away bits and pieces from the run-down sheet.

'We the people.' Interview with Mr. Albert Badrock 3AW 18.8.1951 at 7.30pm. (that sounds like an address from Donald Trump).

Elliot: In tonight's edition of the Koolmint Show, 'We the People,' we're about to meet a hypnotist. That in itself, doesn't sound very alarming, but our guest claims that he can make himself invisible which is quite alarming. Of course, he can only make himself invisible to any of his hypnotic subjects, so our studio audience needn't have any fears that he will vanish in a puff of smoke like Mandrake. An electrician in a big city store, our guest has been giving lunch-time demonstrations for his fellow workers and has achieved some astonishing results. He performs on suburban stages and has given many shows in the aid of charity. He appears under the stage name of 'Mr Alber,' but I want you to give him a welcome under his own name, Albert Badrock.

Applause.

Elliot: Well, before you go off into thin air, Mr Albert, perhaps you'll tell us how you first became interested in hypnosis?

Albert: Tells of amateur experiments at Healesville. Then went on from there for five years of study. (I can only wonder about the experiments and the five years of study as I have all his records relating to his academic achievements and there was no record of studying hypnotic things. I really think he may have read a book or two.)

Elliot: And these lunch hour demonstrations you gave for your fellow workers, what form did they take?

Albert: He tells of getting the office, 'Woman Hater,' to embrace a girl under a hypnotic spell. Also, of how this particular lad was a good subject... could see 'through' the table.

Elliot: and was that where you got the idea of getting people to see through you too? (That's beginning to sound like the host is a little sceptical).

Albert: tells of woman, blank, blank (that's where the silverfish ate bits and pieces).

Elliot: and have you ever done the invisible act with any other subject?

Albert: tells of the sailor and the cigarette. (The mind boggles with that quick reference).

Elliot: Of course, hypnosis is used extensively in medical work, isn't it? (This is where things could have become a little more difficult for my father, bluffing his way through the interview).

Albert: tells of its uses in medical work. (I would have loved to hear about that).

Elliot: Well, I think that now we should have a demonstration of your powers, Mr Albert.

Goes into ten minutes of the hypnotic act.

Elliot: Well, thank you, Mr Alber, we've been most impressed with your ability, and your appearance in the Koolmint Show, 'We the People,' thanks again, Mr Albert Badrock.

Applause,' and in a nutshell that was how my father took over the world of hypnotherapy.

My father, dad, made other references to his short show business career in his life story. Items of interest are attempting to hypnotise a large audience one evening at the Assembly Hall in Collins Street, Melbourne. Both mum and dad had become something of minor celebrities during the early 1950s. Hypnotism was becoming a popular form of entertainment, and if there was a pound to be made, my parents were in it. Hundreds of tickets had been sold and, according to my father's papers, 'a resounding financial success.' Even as I write this, I am still sceptical about the whole process. In one part of my father's papers, he tells of curing a young child who had the misfortune of suffering from a severe case of stuttering. One session with the Amazing Mr Alber and he apparently was cured. On another, my father visited a local ANZ bank manager each Thursday evening for three months. The man had suffered a nervous breakdown from his experiences during the Second World War. After my father's sessions, the man was able to re-enter society and his job with the bank.

I wondered what happened to all this, and the question was solved. Due to criticism from the Catholic Church and other sectors of the community, the practice was deemed to be, 'the work of the devil.' Although my parents were from an Anglican background, they did cease the practice. Not to be dissuaded from all this, my father still felt the need to perform in front of a crowd. What did he do? The Amazing Mr Alber became a magician. He haunted the many magic shops that were in business in Melbourne and, although he wasn't flushed with funds, took care when examining many of the tricks, and then made the items himself. This brings me to one more of the magic episodes much later in his life.

A few years before he departed this world, his desire to examine the mysteries of magic, he thought it would be interesting to see how a guillotine was made and how he could construct a working model. Not a full-size one, but one that could be carted around his local area and shown as part of his magic routine. He had recently been introduced to the internet and this opened a new and exciting facet of his life. Rather than hobbling down to the local library to find what he was looking for, he explored the secrets of the guillotine online.

Having been retired from his working life for many years, a combination of his age and his lack of mobility due to a few ongoing health issues, he was 'confined to barracks.' This allowed him to toil away in his garage unhindered by my mother and others. After several weeks, the model was ready for an official unveiling. Both my parents were members of the Flinders Probus Club. My father's guillotine stood proudly in the garage and was around a metre high. A solid steel blade was mounted to the frame, and for all intents and purposes, it appeared to look like a genuine guillotine except a miniature version.

Would it work? Of course, it would. He proudly placed a carrot into the hole, locked down the mechanism, released the catch at the top and down came the blade. With a blink of the eyelid, the front part of the carrot fell into the small basket. "Let's have a go at a bigger veggie," said my father. Same process, and same result.

Well, both my wife and I were impressed. But the big test would be in front of the Flinders Probus Club members. He proposed that he give the audience something that they would remember for ever. He explained his idea to the committee of the club, and even went as far as to suggest one of the members would be able to place one of their hands in the frame below the blade and see if it worked. The committee said they would discuss the proposal and let him now before their next meeting.

Under no circumstance would the Amazing Mr Alber be able to perform the exhibition of his guillotine in front of the club. Due to the danger of the act. Speaking to my father later, he was extremely disappointed with their decision. Of course, the mechanism was totally safe as he did pull apart the frame and explain how the blade could not sever even a leaf as there was a fool proof bolt to stop the 'execution.' The blade had been designed to bypass the object and simply appear to pass through and that was the end of his magic career.

Being on the internet then, he offered the guillotine free to a magician who was willing to collect it from Hastings. A young magician drove down from Queensland, thanked my father, and took it back for a new life in the sunshine state. Did I stick my arm in the bottom of the guillotine and let him sever my hand off? No bloody way.

Chapter 24

Anyhow, after that short diversion it's back to the Voyager of The Seas and the hypnotist show. The Royal Theatre was almost to capacity, the lights went down, and our cruise director once again bounced onto the stage and introduced the man of the moment. He went through his spiel and then invited those who wished to be hypnotised onto the stage. Within an instant, close to twenty passengers made their way up and onto the seats that had been already lined up on stage.

A diverse group they were. It wasn't long before the group had settled into the act and were ready for their fifteen minutes of fame. Given that this was his second performance on the cruise, some of those on stage had experienced the act before and were keen to play a part again. Call me cynical but one person, and she was first up and the first to appear to go under his spell, must have been the first into the theatre as soon as it was open, as she was seated as close to the stage as possible. As if by a divine decree, she was seated on her chair and immediately flopped down like a rag doll under his magic spell. At the other end of the line, a lady of Asian background was the complete opposite. Dressed like she was off to meet the Queen, high heels and all, after a third of the way through the performance, several of the others were permitted to return to their seats. While she was left onstage to either make up the numbers or she might have been a friend of the hypnotist.

We lasted to the end of the performance, which was quite a feat for us, as we have known to beat a hasty retreat when enduring performers who were in the process of boring us to sleep. Another act over and it was time to return to the Pig and Whistle for a quiet drink in preparation for our next port in the morning, Tauranga. We began talking to a lovely young couple from the outback Queensland town of Richmond.

Keagan and Lorraine were the owners and operators of the town's butcher shop. This was their first holiday in over two years. His father oversaw the local abattoir, and although the region had been suffering through a long drought, recent rains had given their industry a boost.

According to the town's profile on the internet, the population only numbers approximately six hundred and fifty. The town is situated four hundred and ninety-eight kilometres from Townsville and four hundred and six kilometres east of Mt Isa. So, you could say, it's in the middle of nowhere. We enjoyed their company, and in our opinion, they were two young Australians, out in the middle of nowhere having a real go. If we get the opportunity to call into Richmond while dragging our caravan up their way in the future, we said, we'd call in and say hello.

The next morning was going to be our second port of call with our amended schedule. Having been twice in the town, firstly, over forty-three years ago on our honeymoon and, secondly, a few years back on another cruise. We were looking to see a different side to the town and trying to find a real cup of coffee.

First things first. The Port of Tauranga is right alongside the main business hub of the town. Essentially, we walked off the ship, through the secure port area and onto Salisbury Avenue, walk a hundred metres, if that, and turn left onto Maunganui Road and follow all the other cruise passengers. One thing before we made our way along those two streets, we stopped at the first corner outside the port area. Strategically placed immediately on the right is the Tauranga Information and Booking Centre. Right outside were, three of those exceptionally large, three-wheel motorbike trikes. Big things they were. I suspected that my wife would have loved to go for a half hour tour around on the back of one of those things. I said, "how about we lash out and go for a spin?" We went in, paid our money, and were assigned one of those big hairy things, and that wasn't just the trike.

Our guide was a local, who was passionate about his town and his job. Tall with long hair in a ponytail and attired like he could have been a bikie. Looks can be deceiving as it was with our guide. Polite and well-spoken, he welcomed us to Tauranga and explained where we were going. "No helmets needed?" I asked. "No, according to the local registration people, this vehicle is considered a motor car and not a bike." I certainly thought it looked like a motorbike trike, sounded like a trike and we were sitting at the rear with our hair being blown off our scalps. According to our knowledgeable guide, and now best friend for the next half an hour, the machine has a large Chevrolet engine and gearbox so that qualified it as a motor vehicle. We really couldn't have cared less as we were having a ball.

Of course, there was the obligatory stop for a photo opportunity along the wonderful stretch of beach beside Marine Parade. Our photo shows us with smiles, wind-blown hair, and a look on our faces as if to say, 'are we really doing this?' As our tour made its way around the town and the beachfront, we were becoming aware that the area was one of the growth areas of the North Island. Multi-million-dollar houses dominated the area especially along Marine Parade.

It wasn't long before our tour came to an end, we jumped off, well to be honest, rearranged ourselves, hobbled off and thanked our guide. Our next mission was to find a decent cup of coffee. One last question to our new best friend, 'where can we find a real cup of coffee in this town?'

The place to go was a short walk back down Maunganui Road and find a café named, Eighty-Eight Café. And off we went. Of course, it was down the other end of the road, but it didn't really matter, as we had the entire day to ourselves. Café found, and in we went. The café was small, vibrant, and doing a roaring trade. A couple of other cruise ship passengers were there, obvious because they were still wearing their cruise cards around their necks. We made our way down through the tiny café, past the counter and found a small table in the rear courtyard. Surrounded by old bricks and timber walls, the area was almost full of happy patrons. I left my wife, well not really, it just sounds that way, and went back inside and ordered our two mugs of extra strong cappuccinos, and a decadent caramel slice to be shared. It wasn't long before our coffees and slice were delivered to our table. The staff were fantastic; polite and attentive. Sitting under the rows of clear light bulbs, surrounded by aged brick and timber walls, it was no wonder the delightful café was so popular. To use an old cliché, 'it was with a heavy hand on our heart we had to leave.' There was far more of Tauranga that needed to be explored. And we were off and back down to the beach.

It wasn't long before we made our way to the start of the walk onto Moturiki Island, previously known as Leisure Island. This unique part of the world is a small island located a few metres from the sand, and I would imagine when the tide was in, the whole land mass would become isolated from the mainland. The part that did get our attention was the remains of the area known as Marineland, Moturiki. From a bit of research from the Tauranga Historical Society, the area on the island was developed in 1965. A local entrepreneur had the idea to create a large outdoor aquarium on the island's old quarry site. Blasting and drilling proceeded to create a large pool area where dolphins and other aquatic marine life would be the star attractions. But with all good ideas, some things are just not meant to last with time.

With the deaths of several dolphins and other animals, questions were raised, and the viability of the enterprise was questioned. In 1981 the site was closed and sold. Now all that remains are large areas of concrete being reclaimed by nature, and if we hadn't noticed a couple of signs detailing the past, we wouldn't have a clue to its history.

Lunch time was beckoning, so back to the main shopping and retail area on Maunganui Road. We had noticed on our earlier morning visit a place right next to the Eighty-Eight Café. Astrolabe Brewbar looked appealing. We wandered in and it was packed to the rafters. I think an appropriate description would be, 'Quirky and funky New Zealand bar and bistro.'

A table found, a menu located, it was time to order. I made my way over to the counter to place our order. "Before I take your order, sir, I need to tell you what we don't have available today for lunch. Due to a big night last night, and to be honest, we didn't know a cruise ship would be docking, we have quite a limited menu, what would you like?" I would have thought word would have got out into the local hospitality businesses that three and a half thousand tourists were going to descend into their town. We certainly knew where we were going, maybe it was a breakdown in communication somewhere. But anyhow, we both ordered the salt and pepper calamari with chips and salad. It duly arrived, with an apology, "sorry, we didn't know a cruise ship was coming in, but enjoy your lunch." And so, we did. Crisp, hot, and spicy, just how it should be.

After lunch, what to do? We had crammed in a fair bit since this morning, I casually suggested to my wife, "would you like to go for a bit of a walk?" "Ok, where were you thinking?" she replied. "How about we do the circuit around Mt Manganui, it shouldn't be too difficult?" To quote a famous Badrock saying, 'is this going to be a good idea, or will there be a divorce on the way?'

It was only a leisurely fifteen-minute walk to the start of the circuit. About a kilometre or so, slightly uphill. When we approached the actual start of the circuit, I asked my wife, "are you sure you wish to continue, we can always turn around and go back to the ship?" "No, I think I'll be fine, let's just start and get it over with." And with those words of encouragement, we began the circuit. I did notice a discrete sign saying the walk was two thousand two hundred and fifty metres and should only take approximately forty-five minutes. From my bit of research, I have since found a couple of more details that either we didn't notice or plainly missed.

Firstly, according to the official local website, the distance is three thousand five hundred metres and should take a leisurely forty minutes to complete. And secondly, there was a bit of a landslide back in April 2017. Care should be taken or so it said. So off we went on our little stroll around Mt Maunganui. According to the short guide at the beginning of the circuit we were at least heading in the right direction, clockwise.

As we made our way along the first part of the track, the Voyager of The Seas could be seen gracefully resting, if that's what ships do while in port, far away in the distance. Once out of our sight the track began to wind its way around the coastline.

After what seemed an eternity, maybe twenty minutes or so, a detour sign was across the track blocking our progress. And there it was. The temporary set of steps. I immediately began to look for the base station of the chairlift. They were so steep and had the appearance of having been in place for an awfully long time. Grass and weeds were growing profusely between the gravel that had been lodged between the timber risers. I did the only thing that mattered at the time. I asked my wife, "should we turn around and return, rather than have the need to conquer these bloody steps?" "There is no way I'm going back, I am sure we must be over halfway, so just keep going."

After hauling our way up those steps, they even appeared to be steeper going down the other side. Even I was becoming a little fatigued as we had already been walking for several hours if you include our morning's expedition. On and on we went, but a curious thing was beginning to happen. Other walkers, and would you believe, joggers seemed to be giving us a wide berth. I don't think we were, 'on the nose,' I think the realisation of the coronavirus publicity was beginning to cause people to consider maintaining the one and a half metres of separation.

Eventually, we rounded the last bend and the town re-emerged into view. It appeared that we could almost touch the vista in front, but a reality check brought everything back into perspective. A small sign announcing, 'only one and half kilometres to park entrance.' "Would you like me to carry you?" I asked in sympathetic tones. "No, just put me into a ball shape and roll me back down the hill, I'm absolutely stuffed," was her reply.

After what seemed an eternity, the end was denoted by a small gate and entrance through the caravan park. Things were becoming a little thirsty. The first place open was one of those small convenience stores, small variety, but top price for two bottles of water. Then the final slog to the ship, but in this case, it felt like the final leg to the South Pole. Several pit stops later, the last being just a hundred metres to the secure area of the port. "Do we need to call for an ambulance?" I mumbled to myself. One and a half hours after we left approximately the same location, we stumbled through security, were squirted twice with hand sanitizer before we reboarded the ship. Within a couple of minutes, we were whisked back up to the rarefied air of the Royal Caribbean Lounge up on deck fourteen. A drink in hand, I casually asked my wife, "why did you agree to walk around Mt Manganui after our morning's walk?" Her reply, "Since you agreed to take us for a ride on the motorbike trike, I felt it only fair that I should do something that you wanted to do." Isn't life a wonderful thing?

Back up on deck fourteen, it was business as usual. It seemed that a lot of passengers didn't feel the need or desire to get off and discover the delights of Tauranga and Mt Manganui. Down below on the pool deck a familiar scene was occurring. But this time with a different cast. In one of the large spa pools, four large, and I mean very large, men of Middle Eastern appearance were inhabiting a spa. All had their arms out on the edge, arms almost touching, but with the serious appearance which implied, 'keep out, do not enter.' While in the swimming pool on the starboard side, one large and imposing male was strutting toward the pool's edge. He looked like a man with a Polynesian background. Tall, well-built, and sporting a long ponytail. He entered the water and then proceeded to swim breaststroke up and down in the middle of the pool. It was one of those 'look at me, aren't I a magnificent specimen of a male?' I immediately thought, 'you look a bit like a wanker,' but who was I to judge, seated in my lofty eyrie up on deck fourteen?

We had forsaken our prime seats and returned to our stateroom, or as we called it, 'our cabin.' A quick change of clothes, a bit of a quiet reflection on our day, and then back up to the Royal Caribbean Lounge to prepare mentally for dinner. When we returned, of course we had been relegated back to the third row of seating, and this was right next to the timber dance floor. Fortunately, no one was doing a dance class, thank god, but there was a lady playing a Flamenco guitar at full throttle, so it wasn't too bad a place to be seated. Two ladies did get our attention and they were seated on the other side of the railing. They both appeared to be desperate for someone to talk to. As we say in Australia, 'done up to the nines.' They seemed to be in their late 50s. Karen struck up a polite conversation about the day's activities, while I did my best to hear what they were saying. The interesting thing was, that both ladies' partners, I would presume husbands, who could have been two of those men, who were earlier sitting in one of the spa pools had just joined them. If you can think back to the movie, 'Men in Black,' mean-looking all dressed in black with an attitude to match, that's how they appeared. No smiling, no talking, just sitting there staring into space. Well, I can only think their households could have been completely the opposite of ours.

That evening we were shown to our table for dinner and were seated next to a lovely English couple from Kent. As the conversation flowed, we discovered that they had flown from England to Melbourne and their trip was for six weeks. They had hired a car in Melbourne, driven via the Princess Highway through the recent bushfire areas and onto Sydney. Their goal was to visit the fabled South Pacific. To say they were disappointed was an understatement but, as they said, "well, we haven't been to New Zealand before, so it won't be a total waste of time."

<h1 style="text-align:center">Chapter 25</h1>

At the crack of dawn the next morning, we arrived in the beautiful North Island region of The Bay of Islands. The Voyager of The Seas, as are all other cruise ships who visit the area, is required to anchor off the coast of Waitangi and transport their passengers via the ship's tenders. The process involved in moving three and a half thousand passengers off the ship in an orderly fashion is a marvellous thing. The tender boats are capable of seating close to one hundred and fifty or so. A tender ticket is required and then you are asked to wait in a lounge and then wait for your number to be called. We were then instructed to follow the directions down to deck two and pass through the security system, have our cruise cards scanned, and then we were ushered aboard. Talk about how it would be to be a sardine, we could only imagine. For some odd reason, only a couple of the windows were open, it was extremely hot, and the trip took close to half an hour. Eventually, the small pier at Waitangi came into view. Could you believe it? There was a queue of small orange boats like ours all bobbing around like corks in a bucket. Some waiting to depart while the others were waiting in line to unload their passengers. It was now becoming unpleasantly hot, so there was nothing else to do but sit tight, which wasn't a problem, and just be patient.

Eventually, it was our time to get off and out and away from the maddening crowd. A fleet of buses were waiting at the jetty car park and in no time, we were on our way to the nearby town of Paihia. I can only imagine what this beautiful seaside village must be like without the constant stream of visitors primarily from cruise ships. The town does appear to have a lot of holiday accommodation, so it must be popular throughout the year.

The buses stop in the centre of the town, right outside the Visitor Information Centre. Directly over the road is the retail hub, and what seems a permanent market. I was quite sure that the same stall holders were there on our previous trip several years back. A quick wander around the market looking at things we really didn't need and then back over the road to Fuller's Ferry Service to purchase a couple of tickets for the ride over to the historic town of Russell. There were two options for the ferry, one the 'fast' ferry, and the other, you guessed it, the 'slow' ferry. We really didn't care which one but fortunately the 'Fast' one was about to dock. Our tickets in hand, we followed instructions from the captain and made our way to our seats. Fifteen minutes was the prescribed travelling time across the bay to the historic town of Russell. Although we had been fortunate to have visited this beautiful part of New Zealand before it always carried its own special form of magic and on this occasion, the magic was still there. A beautiful day to be motoring across the bay and heading for Russell. The Voyager of The Seas was off in the distance silhouetted by the surrounding ocean, but this time, framed by blue skies and a flotilla of yachts in the foreground.

As the ferry neared the Russell Pier, there were hundreds of other visitors already wandering the foreshore, poking their noses into the open doors of shop fronts, wallowing in the waters in front of our destination. The Duke of Marlborough Hotel. Still sitting there majestically on the waterfront. Having waited a few years for this lunch there was no way we weren't going to get a seat. It was a little after noon so the doors were open. Dozens of diners had already grabbed the prime seats on the balcony overlooking the bay. Waiting patiently to be shown to a table by the ever-efficient doorman, it wasn't long before we were escorted out onto the balcony. We couldn't believe it. The same table right on the front left-hand side of the balcony. There was only one thing to do, order the same meals as previously. As the rest of the Badrock family would know, it was freshly-caught fish, battered to perfection and chips to die for. A small fresh salad completed the dish. Only one more thing to complete this scene of tranquillity and bliss, a glass of New Zealand's sauvignon blanc.

Almost as soon as our order had been taken, it felt like the rest of the passengers from the Voyager of The Seas found where we were sitting. Some were parts of large groups, while others like us, thought we could find a bit of space after being cooped up on the ship. We sat there as long as possible soaking up the atmosphere and thinking, 'god, this is a beautiful part of the world.'

Eventually, we felt the need to share our prime position, so it was time to pay the bill and find a decent cup of coffee. After wandering around the two lovely, large lounge areas of the hotel, I noticed a small bar area out through one of the lounges. I felt like we had to creep in as it seemed to be 'staff only.' I asked the bar staff, "any chance we can order a couple of strong cappuccinos?" "Of course, sir, please take a seat on the couches over there and I'll bring them over to you shortly." We turned around to find several of those old, but extremely comfortable, leather chairs that swallow you up as soon as you sit down. We watched the waiters and waitresses going about their business, while we waited for our coffees.

It wasn't long before our coffees arrived and another session of watching the world go by. As they say, all good things must end, so it was a bit disappointing that we had to leave the comfort of the bar at the Duke of Marlborough Hotel and amble back to the jetty for the ride back to Paihia. One final thing was to have a quick stop into the local hall just down from the hotel and have a peek inside. The locals host a small market of hand-made items from wood-carvings to other items such as sewing stuff. I use that term lovingly of course, as my wife has a passion for anything to do with material, sewing and quilting. I took the noble option to have a short look inside, then mentioned, "take your time, I'll have a wander around the area."

After what seemed an eternity, well, not really, but there is only so much looking and photographing in the small park alongside the hall. We eventually met again, "are you happy with what you purchased?" I asked. "Of course, I felt the need to support my fellow sewers."

By a stroke of luck, I noticed there was one of the tiniest supermarkets in all the world right next door to the park. Still desperate to purchase a small bottle of coffee and take it back to the ship, we went in and found the smallest and most expensive bottle of coffee known to man. A bit of a problem as we didn't have an electric jug kettle in our cabin. "Not a problem, I'll just take it into the dining room and put it on the table," said my much better half, and so she did.

We made our way back along the road and headed to the jetty for the return trip back to Paihia. In the now blazing sun, the queues had already begun to snake back from the ramp leading down to the next ferry. Without waiting, I was on a mission, I urged my wife to follow me and not get distracted by the tourist brochures in the small building on the jetty. A ferry was nearing the end of the jetty and, from my astute reckoning, I thought we should just about make it on. Of course, having already waited for close to half an hour, it felt like we needed to push some others off who were in the line in front of us.

Having a polite conversation with anyone willing, we all agreed that Russell was a wonderful place to spend the day, but the novelty of all this queueing was beginning to wear off.

As our line of passengers made its way towards the ferry, we thought we were in with a chance to get on. But you guessed it right. The official bean counter ahead of us held up her hand and said, "sorry, that's all for this ferry, the rest of you will need to wait for the ferry that will be here soon." Great, we were still standing there in the blazing sun, watching the 'fast' ferry depart the dock and head for the open waters of the bay. It wasn't too long before things were beginning to improve. As was the line of other passengers who were now streaming towards the jetty. We were at the front of the queue and couldn't really care less about the others behind us. A bit selfish but we had now been waiting for close to fifty minutes.

As the ferry neared its position, we could clearly see that this wasn't the 'fast' ferry. If you could imagine one of those old-style pleasure boats you would find in the Lake District in England, then that's what this one looked like. Small, squat and rounded with the wheel-house sitting proudly up the front, or as I should correctly say the bow. The rear or stern section was open to the elements, but did have the advantage of a small-rounded roof section. The section was enclosed, while we chose a seat on the port-side along the wheelhouse. Seating was still a prime object of those still stranded on the jetty. We were surprised at how many passengers this little boat could carry.

As we slowly shuddered away from our little piece of New Zealand paradise, it was a relief to be finally underway. There is a restriction of five knots when motoring through the immediate area, so it was one of those moments, to quote an Australian movie, 'you can feel the serenity.' Clear water and a gentle breeze only enhanced the experience. Once out of the five-knot area, did our little ferry accelerate towards to goal of Paihia? It felt like we were going backwards. Fish and the occasional sea slug were moving faster than we were.

Immediately to my right, a small group of European backpackers were preening themselves on the front, raised section of the bow. Not a care in the world, enjoying the sun, basking in their own elated position in the world, but as I am writing this, the world is in the constant grip of the Coronavirus pandemic. I often think about how this small group of friends and travellers coped on the remainder of their journey.

Enough of that, let's get back to the 'slow boat to China,' or in this case, Paihia. As we floated back to the jetty, we could hear our fellow passengers talking among each other about the pace of our return trip. It didn't really matter to be honest, as you know when things are going according to some form of plan. There always needs to be a plan somewhere, as without direction, life's journey can become a bit clouded.

Back on dry land, we made our way to the pickup point for the return bus trip to Waitangi. Joined with hundreds of others, all with the same plan, it wasn't long before the cavalcade of buses arrived. We found a couple of seats at the front so it would be easy get off the bus, walk straight onto the pier and make our way straight onto the waiting tender boat.

Of course, that didn't happen. As we neared the area where the buses were stopping then turning around for another trip, hundreds of waiting passengers could be seen idly standing in line in the blazing sun. "Mm, this might take a while," I said to my wife. "Oh well, at least they're handing out plastic glasses of water, so I think I'll survive." We got into line and waited and waited. A what seemed to be snail pace, as each tender boat departed with its container of sardines, we eventually reached the shade of the covered area of the pier.

After almost an hour of being very patient, our time had finally arrived to board our little orange craft. Jammed in again, but fortunately one of the crew thought to open the front sliding window to allow a bit of fresh air into the boat. All our fellow passengers seemed to have a look of, 'here we go again, let's get this transfer back to the ship as soon as possible.'

As we were making our way off our little boat, a family group in front was too good to ignore. The parents, maybe in their early fifties, even pushing the late fifties, certainly set the precedent for the rest of their family. The father figure, shortish, stocky, would be an apt description, dressed in black, covered in tattoos and the image was finished off with a natty, black Fedora hat. His three-day growth was accompanied by one of those large, thick gold chains around his thick neck. His wife, a bleached blond, with too much bleach, could have done the job herself, was dressed also in matching black. Tight tee shirt, and sporting those tight, 'active wear' tights. They were almost as tight as the skin on her face. There wasn't a smile to be found with either of them.

As for their daughter, well, was she a piece of work. Smallish, all dressed in black, long blonde ponytail, pulled back so tight that it gave her a look of total shock. Eyes bulging out, ears straining to stay attached and all finished off with a vast array of tattoos. Her boyfriend or partner, the only thing larger than all his muscle-bound body was his bulging ego. He was one of the strutters in life. Look at me, don't I look like every woman's object of desire. The baseball cap on backwards, the tightest black singlet known to man, and I would think, several sizes too small. Maybe he had a bad experience in the laundry and managed to shrink it that way. Of course, his shorts were black, on the other hand, there weren't those tight ones, but wide and floppy. This could have been so it would be easier for all those hundreds of leg exercises, but I had my doubts. We both thought, 'you are a wanker, have you looked in the mirror lately?'

As we made our way to the twelfth deck for a bit of a rest from those in the lounge above, we realised it was reasonably pleasant out of the wind, lying on a sun lounger. The ship was in the process of getting ready to depart from Waitangi. It was obvious that many others had chosen not to seek the serenity of being off the ship but had joined others around the swimming pools and spas.

We found our position along the port-side of the deck, right in front of the running track. People were still obsessed with this mindless pursuit they should have taken a breather and had a quick look over the railing to see what was unfolding in front of their eyes.

Right below where we were seated, an older male, maybe late 60s, felt the urge to change out of his swimming shorts. Not the Adonis type at all, but highly overweight, short and bald on top. It never ceases to astound me what some people will do. There he was, what's even more tragic was that he had been wearing a small pair of budgie smugglers, the type that should only be worn by life-savers and Olympic swimmers.

I thought at the time, 'for god's sake, you're not going to get changed out of your bathers in front of all these people, are you?' And that's what he did. With all the skill and tact of a lion tamer being circled by a pride of lions, he wrapped one of those blue towels around his considerable girth, bent over and squirmed out of his bathers. Did he feel the need to first put on a shirt? Of course not, this was his show. It was like watching the world in slow motion, I couldn't believe this was happening in front of all these passengers.

No one seemed to be looking, apart from one elderly lady sitting in the row behind him, maybe she was getting more 'bang for her buck.' After the show was finished, he casually left the stage and I suspect was quietly clapped by his one, new admirer.

After all that excitement, it was getting time to prepare for our evening's activities. Dinner was much the same as all the previous nights, except that I appeared to order the wrong dishes. A prime example of this was my wife ordered the steak, while I asked for the garlic prawns. Hers looked divine, while my three prawns had been on a starvation diet. My three had been severed down the spine to give the effect that there was more on the plate and splayed in half. I poked around trying to find what was inside the shell but all to no avail. "Oh well, maybe dessert will be better," I whispered to my wife.

Dessert was duly delivered. My wife's cheese plate looked the same as all the others that we had tried on the previous evenings, but I chose the Bombe Alaska. Light and fluffy, gently torched by a flame and sitting on a biscuit base with cherries. That is essentially a Bombe Alaska. I had noticed others being delivered to tables in our vicinity, and they looked fantastic. That is one clue when dining on a ship, have a look around on other tables as you make your way to your seats. We call it 'a sneaky peak.'

As our waiter arrived, things didn't look too good. "Please, sir, if this isn't to your liking, we will exchange it for another," he explained. I took one look at what was on the plate and quietly said to my wife, "it's either been dropped and then stood on, on the way from the kitchen, or it's someone's finished dessert." To explain my situation, it should be noted that, immediately it was placed in front of me, the head waiter raced over and apologised profusely for the dish. "So sorry, sir, would you like another one?" What was on my plate were the remains of something which in another incarnation could have been a Bombe Alaska. A creamy, flat mushy mess sitting on a soft and soggy conglomeration of crumbs.

We both looked at each other and said, "I think that's it for the evening there is no coming back for more tonight." And with those profound words, we excused ourselves and left the dining room.

There was only so much entertainment to be endured on a cruise ship. We had a look into the area that houses the vast, expansive gymnasium and both decided that all that exercise would be bad for us, so gave that a miss and headed back down to the Pig and Whistle Bar. A quiet white wine together with a bit of good conversation with another couple our age and then it was time to retire for the evening.

The next couple of days and nights were spent heading in a south-westerly direction for the southern New South Wales coastal town of Eden. Up in our favourite position on deck fourteen, we had a bird's-eye view of where we were heading. The weather on this day had become inclement and the swimming pools were emptied and taped off. The ship was experiencing a fair degree of rolling due to us heading directly into a southerly front.

Another benefit of all this inclement weather was to send the smokers down to deck four, but when we ventured down for an attempt at doing a bit of walking out of the weather, one short trip out into the smokers' fog was enough to send us back to the sanctuary of the Royal Caribbean Lounge, up with the birds. Well, the ones we were sitting near, were more like a flock of old parrots. Three elderly ladies, enjoying their morning coffees, complaining about their families and their lives in general. Families, friends and husbands were the topics of their conversations.

The spa pools were the only places for children to be playing in when the conditions were so bad. Two groups of older primary school kids were trying to create their own whirlpools. Spinning around in constant circles, to speed up the water and then float around in circles.

It was fortunate that I had maintained my intake of sea sickness tablets. We were really 'rocking and rolling' as it's said, the bow of the ship would one moment be facing the sky, then a few seconds later would be pointing at the water. Suddenly there was an enormous collision with something in the water. No one seemed to be concerned, maybe it was a whale or something manmade. We will never know, but we ploughed on regardless.

Immediately beside us were an odd couple. She, the size, and shape of a Japanese Sumo wrestler, and he, her long-suffering husband, dressed conservatively. He sported a neat and tidy red beard, stared blankly ahead and really had the appearance that said, 'I would like to be anywhere else but here.' She was sitting in front of one of the small round glass tables, transfixed with thousands of coloured beads. On the table she had placed a small rectangular light box. I presume this was to enable to see a pattern through the surface on what she was working on.

Clasped between her short, thick stubby fingers was a small set of tweezers. Carefully each little bead was checked, assessed, and then placed into position on top of the panel. I wanted to ask her, 'what on earth are you doing, can't you see your husband has died of boredom?' But no, we just pretended this was not happening as there was another couple who had just sat on the other side of us.

From what we gathered, it looked like mother and son. She, our age, dressed conservatively, while he had the appearance of being the son of God. Late twenties, dark trousers, an old tatty long-sleeved shirt and thongs on his feet. The startling thing was, he did not smile or show any emotion. His appearance was completed with long shoulder-length hair, and a beard to match. Of course, the obligatory dark sunglasses were planted on the end of his nose. I fleetingly thought he could have been blind, but that was soon dispelled when he nodded to his poor mother and then wandered back from where he had crept out from.

Could this scene become any more interesting? Yes, of course it would. The bloody line dancing course began at four p.m. sharp. Dozens all arrived en masse. At the time of writing this, it would have been a wonderful idea if social distancing had been enforced. The buggers were too loud and far too close for our liking, but I suppose we cannot help bad luck.

It was beginning to feel a lot like, 'Ground Hog Day,' another night in the dining room except that, on this evening, it was the second 'formal night.' As on the previous formal night, we tried to try to dress for the night. When we made our way into the dining room again, the standard appeared to have dropped to a new low. From my estimate, and I have been known to get these things wrong on a regular basis, I would think no more than thirty percent of passengers in the dining room were dressed up for the evening. The remaining passengers thought it appropriate to wear anything from tee shirts and shorts, tight 'active wear,' dark sunglasses and their phones stuck under their noses. Why on earth do some people find the need to wear sunglasses inside, and on a bloody cruise ship?

We struck up a conversation with a lovely older couple at our table. Sometimes I think it is best to not say too much about yourself, but in this case, we couldn't get a word in. They had been members of the Salvation Army for all their married life. We heard about their time as missionaries in the South Pacific and all the other places they had been posted to. This was all very commendable, and the world should appreciate their efforts, but really, it all became a little wearing after an hour.

Chapter 26

As we headed towards our last port, Eden, the weather had the appearance of moderating, or was it just an illusion? The pools were refilled, and the strutters and posers found their way back to the favourite positions on the pool deck. We, on the other hand, sought the sanctuary of the Royal Caribbean Lounge once again. We thought at the time that the novelty of spending over seven days at sea was really becoming a bit of a chore.

The only thing that diverted our attention was the goings-on down on the pool deck. The latest offering was four young passengers of Asian descent. Two couples, all trim, taut and terrific, as 'they say.' The two young women were wearing the skimpiest bikinis known to man. I couldn't help but notice from my seat up in the sky, that their two male partners appeared to be more interested in their electronic devices than their girlfriends. The two young women seemed oblivious to all the other males within fifty metres watching their every move. But at the time, I suspect not.

Shortly after their parade around the deck, a quick dip in the pool, they both returned to their sun loungers. I could not tell whether they noticed their new admirer. Seated immediately on a sun lounger in the row behind, was a man of indeterminate age. Possibly in his late forties, a stalker maybe, but it was obvious to those around he was 'taking in the view.' Lying on his back, arms and legs splayed out like one of those star fish that can be seen in an aquarium, except that this excuse of a male was wearing the smallest of swimming costumes. Know in Australia as, 'budgie smugglers.' The four your passengers ignored their admirer and continued enjoying their own company.

The next morning, the lovely coastal town of Eden was finally reached. Not having visited the town for many years, it would be interesting to see how the area had changed, if anything. I must admit, after all this floating around in the Tasman Ocean, we were excited about the prospect of getting off the Voyager of the Seas.

As we finally came into Eden the thought did cross our minds, 'could we ask any of our family to drive the seven hours over the mountains and pick us up?' Common sense prevailed, but there was always the option of hiring a car and then driving ourselves back to Bright.

We decided to enjoy our last day of the cruise by being two of the very first passengers to get off and see what Eden had to offer. The local Bega Shire had the forethought to commission a new cruise ship wharf. At seventy million dollars, the new wharf was designed to accommodate large ships which would deliver a much-needed financial benefit to the town and the surrounding districts.

Being situated down on the waterfront obviously, the town itself is located up on the surrounding hills. We could have chosen to walk up, but the offer of a free bus shuttle was too good to refuse.

Our host for the short trip into town was one of those ladies who relished the opportunity to showcase her town. As all the sights of Eden passed by, the highlight according to our guide was the small, and recently-renovated Catholic Church. "Does anyone know Saint Mary McKillop?" I cheekily mentioned that, "I thought she was dead." Our guide simply smiled and continued with her summary of the town.

Being desperate once again for a decent cup of coffee, we got off the bus outside the Eden Fisherman's Recreation Club and wandered inside. We signed in as temporary visitors, desperate for both a coffee and the toilet. Having visited lots of these New South Wales clubs over the years, it's always surprising what the visitor comes across. The Fisherman's was no different. A polite lady heavily made up, but still with a welcome smile. The other two males were a lot younger and possibly had been living in Eden for too long. The younger of the two was overly nice, to the point of me thinking, 'for God's sake, stop mincing around and just show us where to go.' While the older of the two was the complete opposite. Overweight, covered in tattoos and sporting one of the hairstyles that should have been left in the 1970s Short, almost shaved sides, and a 'mullet' down to his shoulders. An attitude to match, mean-looking, and it appeared that he did not want to be there.

We found a table away from the entrance, beside the front screened window. A view would have been nice, but I suspected at the time, that management did not think the public should be gazing in at the patrons inside.

We also thought, maybe the sounds and sights of the poker machines whirling away in the far lounge might be a little off-putting to those wandering along the footpath outside. Each to their own I suppose, but the two coffees were delivered with a smile, and that was fine with us.

After our close encounter with the mullet and his side-kick, it was time to explore on foot the sights of Eden. Sometimes the best way we have found to have a poke around a new place is to follow the crowds. On foot that is. Although it seemed that the other three thousand-odd passengers were invading the shops along the main street, many were headed down Mitchell Street towards the foreshore. At the end of Mitchell Street, we turned left and wandered aimlessly along Aslings Beach Road via the fantastic boardwalk.

The sweep of Aslings Beach seemed to stretch out in front of us forever. Beautiful turquoise blue water and sand worth building a castle on. Several of our fellow passengers had taken the easy option of the free bus shuttle service to the beach.

It has always surprised me how some of the best locations in these far-flung places are the site of the local cemetery. If I cast my mind back to some of our earlier trips, a couple of truly magnificent locations spring to mind. Take Norfolk Island, for instance. That little place stuck out in the middle of nowhere, between Australia's east coast and the northern part of New Zealand, has one of the most spectacular and isolated cemeteries you could come across. Located right beside the windswept ocean, surrounded on one side by a row of ancient Norfolk Pine trees, and a steep ridge on the other. The cemetery commands everyone's attention who take the time to wander through the perimeter fence and amble among the ruins. The cemetery is still in use, so those who are buried in this sacred place will be keeping company with long-forgotten convicts, and more recent notables such as Colleen McCulloch.

One of those other cemeteries that come to mind that we have wandered through, and that has a wonderful vista for those buried there, is the one in Tasmania. Sitting beside the beach, below The Nut at Stanley on the far north-west coast, in prime seaside position, a short walk from the centre of the historic town, it too reeks of times gone past. Gravestones over a hundred years of age leaning at angles that cry out, as if to say, 'I'm over here, come and support me, as none of my relatives can remember my name.'

A small, rickety timber fence is all that separates the living from the dead. At least the view makes the location one to reflect on one's own mortality. Enough of that sentimental rubbish, it's time to get back to reality, and the story at hand.

Of course, we just had to make our way through the front gate of the cemetery at Eden. Most of our fellow passengers were making their way directly off the shuttle bus and were heading straight for the nearby timber boardwalk. A quick ponder at the signs explaining the historic virtues of the area and the beach, and they were all off in different directions. We, on the other hand, wandered around soaking in bits and pieces of the history lying below our feet. I don't know about you, but both Karen and I try not to stand directly over someone's grave. A bit difficult when you consider that in most old, established graveyards, the graves are jammed in side-by-side. I wouldn't have thought land was an issue when the cemeteries were originally designed. We found the location just as profound as the other two cemeteries that I have just mentioned. A nice place to visit, but not a place to reside.

Anyhow, we stood and gazed out to sea and tried to imagine what it must have been like for those early settlers who travelled halfway around the world by sailing ship and then slammed directly into the many headlands and reefs that surround the Australian coastline.

The idea was to slowly walk back to the centre of Eden via the boardwalk. That was the plan, except that the tiny refurbished Our Lady Star of the Sea Catholic Church got in the way. We have always felt the urge to wander into some of those small country churches when the front door is open. On this occasion, the front door to the old church was open and welcoming visitors.

Not being overly religious, I can only guess where this disinterest stems from. Maybe it was all those Sunday mornings many decades ago, when as young children, we were dragged kicking and screaming to church on most Sunday mornings. What was even worse was the need of my mother to think an extra hour of Sunday School would hold me in good stead for the rest of my life. As we hear constantly today, 'too much of a good thing can be bad for you,' I think that was the problem. Well, it sounds good to me anyway.

The Our Lady Star of the Sea Catholic Church did have a remarkably interesting story to tell. Originally constructed on the site in November

1860. The land granted in 1863 for the establishment of a Church Presbytery and School. The whole thing was burnt to the ground by a disastrous fire on the 14th of April 1877.

After the disastrous wreck of the 'Lyee Moon' at the nearby Green Cape, on which one of the victims was the mother of Mary MacKillop, Flora MacKillop in 1886. Young Mary established a school there in the church building. This ran until 1912. Then, Mother Mary Mackillop visited the school on Sunday 26th of March 1901. This, according to the plaque out the front of the building, was to inspect the children and equipment and stated that her visit went on for the next eight days. That must have been a very thorough visit to have taken that long. Her second visit was again in the same year in August.

The old church fell into disrepair for many years, but due to a bunch of very resilient locals thinking the building was worthy of restoration, they decided to get together and restore it to its former beauty. Today its doors are open and provide a wonderful introspect into the life and times of now, Saint Mary MacKillop. One of those precious things that unless we got out of our cars, and in this case a ship, we would have not come across this little gem.

Although the newer church sits on the headland only a few short steps away, nothing can take away the importance of the little old timber church. We made our way in through the brightly-painted red wooden door and had a poke around. A beautiful timber floor with the alter down the front, it was easy to imagine what the church was like when it was being used for its original purpose. Today its restoration reflects both the local Catholic community and the importance that Saint Mary MacKillop meant to the region. The sign above the front door tells all who enter that it's now the Mary MacKillop Museum, and visitors are welcome. When we were wandering around aimlessly reading all the various pieces of information, there were another couple of people inside apart from us. Both my wife and I can never be in the same place in a building that houses anything of historical interest. We have always found our own way around these fascinating places.

For as long as I can remember, both Karen and I have an unwritten understanding that we go our own way and at our own pace. I seem to move around areas that interest me, while my wife has the need to read every single item that is presented. Eventually, we do make landfall together and generally enquire of each other, "did you notice that item over there?" We exchange details then wander off in different directions again. On this occasion, my wife was talking to a lady who seemed to be involved with the museum. Older type, grey hair, light blue cardigan and a neat, pleated shirt. I thought, all we needed was a cup of tea and a couple of scones and we could have been at a CWA meeting and afternoon tea.

Beside her was an older male, who from my observation could have been her husband. Same age, same grey hair, pale neat shirt and recently-pressed trousers. He was holding a few leaflets and looked like he needed to be talking to someone. I made my way over in his direction and asked him about the restoration and the details regarding the history of the church. A very pleasant man, knowledgeable and passionate about the old church.

He then quietly proceeded to tell me the story of the church and its relationship with Australia's newest Saint. At the end of our polite discussion, he went over to a desk and presented me with a calendar detailing all the Saint's days of the year. Maybe my interest was worthy of such a gift, but it was a nice gesture. Something to hang on the toilet wall, maybe not, but an item to cherish if you were a believer.

I continued around the hall taking in all the displays and eventually came to the lady who I have just mentioned. "My God, this is a wonderful display and a credit to all those who gave their time and money for the restoration." She replied, "well, thank you, we all do our bit in the service to our community."

After a bit more polite chit-chat, I made my way around to my wife who was still reading everything that was displayed intently. "Oh, good to see you again, I see you met Sister Mary, wasn't she lovely, and knowledgeable?"

I immediately regretted my 'my God' reference but she appeared to take it in her stride. We eventually made our way back to the front door and placed a few more dollars in the collection box for the ongoing needs of the museum. A place, certainly worthy of a look-in, if you are passing through Eden.

Back outside, it seemed appropriate to walk the short distance and have a look inside the present Catholic Church. Located between the Museum and the more modern Church stood one of those church bells that needed to be rung. Standing proudly on a tall plinth in the shape of a cross, the bell is mounted inside a circular frame overlooking the ocean. A rope was attached to the top of the bell, and was being rung furiously, or should I say, with a great deal of enthusiasm, by a young male passenger from the ship. How did I know? He still was wearing his cruise card around his neck. I have always desired to give a good yank to a rope with a bell attached but have never had the confidence to do so. Maybe it's the thought that by ringing one of those bells, all manner of signals could be given. A fire, a disaster, or a person lost at sea. I waited, but no one came or seemed to care less, maybe the locals are used to tourists grabbing the rope and enjoying the experience.

The rumbling in our stomachs told us that lunchtime had been and gone, but we still needed something to eat. Heading towards two p.m., we dragged ourselves up the quite steep Chandos Street and found Martin's Pie Place on Imlay Street. It looked like the entire passenger list had descended onto the main street. Literally thousands wandering aimlessly all over the town. We grabbed a small table and two chairs outside the Pie Place, well, it was really a bakery, and it was jammed full of customers. I waited patiently in line, and eventually purchased a pie and a salad roll and a couple of cold drinks. There wasn't really much left as it appeared the town didn't expect an additional three thousand people dropping in for the day.

We sat shoulder-to-shoulder with those around us, elbows tucked in and voices quiet. There was really no point, as we were so close to those around us, it would have been in bad taste to burp too loudly, as everyone would have noticed. The crowd was hovering around us, the same as a shark circling a school of bait fish. "Let's go, I can't stand this," I uttered to my wife. The instant we made to move to leave, our chairs were almost whipped out from under our bums, and 'are you finished, can we have your table?'

Struggling back up the hill along Imlay Street, it was like pushing water uphill with a fork trying to walk through the throng of fellow passengers. At the top of the hill over on the left, was the sanctuary of the Eden Killer Whale Museum. It had been over twenty-five years since we had last entered the doors to see 'Old Tom' and the other bits and pieces in the building. The front seems to have an Art Deco façade, more like an old movie theatre, but it appears to work quite well. From a bit of research, the building was once the local cinema, no wonder it looks so good.

One striking feature that has been a more recent addition is the lighthouse. Yes, they constructed a lighthouse on the site. For all intents and purposes, it looks like the real deal. Slightly smaller than you could find on some lonely outpost of the Colony, but with most males I know, the idea of living in some remote light house conjures up romantic times with the love of their lives. But what those pioneers endured for the safety of others out on the oceans of the world, can best be left in the past.

We went inside and came across a wonderful display about the rich maritime history of Eden and the surrounding area. Of course, it was obligatory to see how 'Old Tom the Killer Whale' was travelling since our last encounter. He was still in pride of place, and from my background as a professional signwriter for many years, I was pleased to see that the old hand-painted lettering was still in place. Old Tom still had that look of, 'how on earth am I still in this bloody museum after all these years?' The entire exhibition is a testament to the locals who relish their history and have provided the many items on display.

I had to have a look at the new lighthouse and was pleased to be able to ascend the spiral steps to the viewing area. From what I was able to read, the entire lighthouse was constructed around a segment of original circular cast-iron steps that was found locally. The story goes something like this. The Green Cape Lighthouse was originally constructed in the Ben Boyd National Park in 1883. The concrete light house was one of the first of its kind and the second highest in New South Wales.

Enough of the history lesson, it's time to get back to the present. Someone got wind of the idea to construct a lighthouse for the Eden Museum. By some strange fate, the old lighthouse was decommissioned in around 1992 and a new metal skeleton-framed tower was being built. With the need gone for the old lighthouse, although it has been left onsite, a section of the old original staircase was found at the nearby tip.

When I entered, it really did have the feel and atmosphere of a real lighthouse. Even the light and the associated mechanism is in situ. The visitor can experience the vista from the outside walkway and pretend they are gazing wistfully out to sea in some far distance corner of the earth.

A quick view and we were off and heading back down the series of walkways back to the port area. It wasn't difficult to head back to the ship, we just go in step with other hundreds all heading in the same direction. At the entrance to the secure area, a few cafés and bars were catering to the influx of visitors to the area. We grabbed a table and a couple of chairs and were intent on enjoying the view while having a cold glass of wine. Easier said than done. I walked into the Pier Bar and Bistro, waited in the queue only to find the queue didn't exist, but I needed a number to be served. I watched and waited, and the progress just to reach the counter to grab a number was glacial. I looked at the ladies behind the counter to see if they were still alive. The process was so slow, I gave up and returned to my wife after twenty minutes. "What happened, where are our drinks, and what took you so long to come back with nothing?" I explained my mission and the result was that we made our way back onto the Voyager of the Seas and headed back up to level fourteen for that quiet drink or two.

That was the only real negative to the end of our wonderful day in Eden as it was our last night on board before we made our way back to Sydney. The curse of the last night at sea is you need to have your luggage packed and left outside your cabin before you go to bed. Being the last night, we again made our way to the dining room and waited with bated breath, to be seated. Thankfully, no need to worry, as we were sure the last night on board, the ship's kitchens would go all out to impress the diners. I thought that this time I'll have something that could not possibly go wrong as far as the food was concerned. My wife ordered the chicken with fresh vegetables, and me, I asked for the garlic prawns. From my experience, garlic prawns and rice cannot be 'stuffed up.' Sauté the prawns in butter, oil and garlic, serve on a bed of boiled rice, if you are a little bit more pretentious, a cone shape of rice sitting gracefully beside the prawns.

Either my name had come up in dispatches, or the waiter had a word with the kitchen, but I must have been a marked man. Our lovely waitress who had attended to us on many nights, I think her name was something like, Mingamee. Mingamee was from Malaysia and was looking forward to ending her contract around September. She was telling us a little of her background. She was engaged to a man who was working in Dubai. When they were both back in Malaysia, they were hoping to start up a small retail business together. She had the bluest of eyes, and with a smile to match. I asked her, "what was he like?" "Well, Graham, he seems like a nice man, I hope he is, I really don't know too much about him."

Maybe we are privileged to live where we do and do take a lot for granted. Knowing full-well that we would not see her again, we wished her well in the future and hoped things worked out.

Anyhow, back to the meal. My wife's chicken and vegetables looked okay, but they were bordering on being so cold, they might not have even gone near a stove. She smiled, and then looked over as my main course was being delivered. Three, large, split-in-half prawns with the insides missing. The rice had the appearance of having been plonked onto the plate without the love that you would expect to find on a ship of this quality. I returned the wry smile to my wife, and said, "are you going to eat yours or shall we just make a break for it?"

With those few words, we excused ourselves and headed for the exit. A quick visit to our cabin, I refuse to call it a stateroom, and we packed the majority of our belongings into our cases and then headed back down to the Schooner Bar for one of those last, expensive drinks. Same crowd and the same music, it felt a lot like 'Ground Hog Day.'

It began to dawn on us that it was only a few hours till dawn, so due to the need to be up early and bright for the next morning, we made our way to our cabin and the rear of the ship. For those of you who are interested, our 'stateroom' was number 694. Our bags had already vanished into the bowels of the ship somewhere so, it was time to finally to take one last look out over the railing and head to bed.

<h1 style="text-align:center">Chapter 27</h1>

The plan was to be dressed and ready to depart the Voyager of The Seas as early as possible. Even both of us were a bit bewildered when we were standing with our suitcases at the taxi rank outside the terminal at seven fifteen a.m. There didn't appear to be much fuss around the rising interest in the Corona Virus until we got into the taxi. Our Indian driver told us, "I started my shift at five a.m. and you are my first passengers for the day. This virus has scared all the tourists away from Sydney." It did look noticeably quiet, no one on the streets, hardly another vehicle to be seen, so maybe the 'pandemic' was real after all.

Little did we know at the time that as they say, 'the shit was about to hit the fan' as far the pandemic was concerned. The ship that was about to cause all the fuss in Australia, the 'Ruby Princess' was only another six days away from docking in Sydney. Luckily, we were on our way home to Bright. The only obstacle in our way was the wait at the Sydney Airport.

When we arrived at the airport, the crowds seemed as busy as in the past, people bustling here and there, waiting in the queues to drop their luggage off and then make their way through security. We, on the other hand, must have looked a bit bewildered, as one of those wonderful ladies who seek out lost, older travellers sidled over to us and asked, "do you need a hand to check in?" We gazed over to the Qantas check-in area and couldn't see a soul. My wife is usually right on the ball as far as these issues are concerned.

We were fumbling around in front of one of those self-serve check-in screens when the lovely lady appeared. Without missing a beat, she took our electronic booking sheet and immediately out came our two luggage tags and our boarding passes. A quick smile and a 'thanks' and we are heading over to toss our luggage into the right place. When I think back, and it really wasn't that far back in time, that checking in at an airport used to be a lot more complicated.

On our very first flight together, which was on our honeymoon back in 1976 at Melbourne's Tullamarine Airport, it really did feel like you were doing something incredibly special. Your manners were just as important as the way you were dressed. Today, some passengers have the appearance that could be more suitable for either a beach party or arriving home late from a drunken night out with the boys. Flying to some far-off exotic location, well, in our case New Zealand, did make us feel part of the 'jet set.'

Today, it's grab a bag, toss in a few clothes, check-in online, turn up at the airport and, in some cases, you have already selected your seat, toss your bags onto the baggage shoot, pass through security and make your way down to your departure lounge.

On the other hand, if you are the chosen one, some bugger will spoil your plans. The dreaded security detail. Those peering through the x-ray unit, those manning the metal walk-through to detect the smallest piece of metal, and the worst of all, the person with the explosive wand. "Excuse me, sir, I need to check you for any traces of explosives and the like." Great here we go again, I don't think I look particularly dodgy, but I understand they are only doing their job. But I, like many others, immediately think, 'have I forgotten to take out the rubbish from my firecracker days twenty-five years ago that I might have left in the bottom of my pocket?'

Many times, for some odd reason, I have been asked to remove my shoes, take off my belt and walk through again and then try to put these things back on while the rest of the world edges past, all the time trying to grab my possessions bouncing around at the end of the conveyor belt. No wonder we feel guilty sometimes, 'oh, the joy of flying.' My wife, on the other hand, invariably is pulled up going through the metal detector device. It's usually a piece of jewellery still around her wrist or some such thing. I must admit, one can get the case of, 'she's not with me' syndrome, I'll grab a quick glance and then innocently wander out of the way. 'Where were you when I needed you?' is the invariable question when we gather all our bits-and-pieces and move away to safer locations.

I have fond memories of one of our trips from the Albury Airport. We had checked in with one of those polite people from Virgin, deposited our luggage and proceeded to go through security, "now, have you left anything in your hand luggage before we go through security?" I asked. "Of course not, what could I possibly have left? Everything is in my suitcase."

I thought I would do the noble thing and go through first, of course, the bloody alarm went off. I needed to remove my belt, re-enter and this time, the all-clear was given. More of a nod, but not to be outdone, the bugger with the explosives wand must have been watching. I went through the same process, arms out-stretched, legs apart and a quick wave of his wand and I was given the all-clear. I turned around to see my wife smiling quietly to herself.

She, too, then approached the metal detector frame after placing her carry-on luggage onto the conveyor belt, and bingo! off it squealed. "Madam, you appear to have a pair of scissors in your carry-on bag, please step over here and open your bag." "No, I don't," she replied. "Oh yes you do, please come over here and open your bag for inspection."

I have often marvelled as to what she has stowed away in her handbag. The size does not always reflect the contents, let alone the combined weight. I really am quite convinced there should be a couple of well-disguised bricks in the bottom section. Out came the make-up bag, jewellery bag, assorted small bottles of perfume, glasses case and other things that I have no idea what could have possibly used for. Sometimes it's just not worth knowing. And there, right at the bottom, secreted away in a long-lost alcove was the offender. The smallest pair of nail scissors known to man, or in this case a woman. "Bugger, I completely forgot where they were, can I have them back?" "Sorry, madam, you can collect them on your return to Albury." "Don't worry, they only cost a couple of dollars, I'll buy another pair when I need them." And with that exchange completed, we regained our composure and waited for our flight to be called.

Anyhow, back to the present. The lovely Qantas lady wished us a pleasant trip and wandered off to assist others like us. The next problem was how on earth do we occupy the next five hours at the Sydney Airport before our flight to Albury was called? No amount of peering at the shop windows would satisfy our need for breakfast. That was our first mission, and when one of those cafés, that all look the same, was open, we made a beeline, found a table and ordered breakfast. You would have thought that having spent the previous eleven days eating our way through the ship's menu, we would have tired of food. But no, the food was particularly good, and even quite satisfying. Maybe it was the fact that our breakfast was prepared and cooked while we were waiting which was the secret.

It was a bit odd that I have always found the need to read a newspaper while away and, from our previous experiences at the Sydney Airport, sometimes you can get lucky. There it was, the Melbourne Herald Sun, almost double the price, but who really cared? I brought it, then sat down with my much better half and endured the next five hours or so.

The COVID-19, as it was to be known, had become the topic of saturation news coverage. Although we did manage to escape Sydney when we did, there was a lot to come as far as the pandemic was concerned.

I am not really sure if this is noticeable, but it has been five months since our return from Sydney before I continued this book. Five days after our return, the cruise ship, the 'Ruby Princess' sailed into Sydney and unloaded dozens of affected passengers into the wider community. Our life would not be the same for some considerable time.

As soon as we returned back home into Bright, our lives jumped back into where it was before our cruise. But, and there is always a but, storm clouds were building over the surrounding hills of Bright. The day after we returned, Bright was in the midst of the annual, Brighter Days Festival. You know what this is all about as I have written about this before. But for those of you who haven't a clue what I am talking about, it goes something like this.

Five thousand or so, give or take a thousand of mostly mature-aged people, try to locate those lost years of their early adult years. A local called Jason Reid, and his fellow organisers and a good selection of volunteers, toil away for months before to arrange a magnificent weekend of music, cars and good times in Bright on the March Labour Day weekend.

Over the past years, the event has been held in Howitt Park right in the centre of Bright. It was always inevitable that the event would outgrow its site. This time the event was moved to a recently-developed site adjoining the Pioneer Park. Now renamed 'The Oaks,' it is a wonderful stretch of recently-laid turf almost the size of the adjacent football oval. With a canopy of mature oak and elm trees, the area was most suitable for its maiden event, the Brighter Days Festival.

Being part of the Bright Lions Club I was rostered for the Saturday afternoon program. Our usual selection of offerings was available to those still trying to find their lost youth. It was a great success for all concerned, but the COVID-19 menace was lurking in the bushes on the other side of the delightful Morses Creek.

One of those movers and shakers in the Bright community, and the local representative of the Brighter Days event, thought that the massive sound-stage could be left onsite for another couple of nights. You just never knew who might be passing. With all the earlier bushfires that had been raging through Victoria and New South Wales, the Victorian Government thought the good country folk might like a bit of light entertainment.

It just so happened at the time that the international entertainer, Katie Perry, was performing in Melbourne. It must have been someone's brainwave to approach her management to perform in Bright. And there she was, three days after the recent Brighter Days Festival performing to five thousand people affected in some way by the devastating fires. It did put our little town on the map again, but immediately after, our world shut down.

Chapter 28

Immediately after Katy Perry departed, so did our sense of freedom. The State Government of Victoria decided that enough was enough. The State was shut down as the cases of the pandemic spiralled out of control. No public gatherings, no work unless you were exempted, and 'stay at home' was the direction. In my case, and with so many others in regional Victoria, we hunkered down and did as we were told. What was even more perplexing was no fishing, no surfing and definitely, no golf.

As far as golfers are concerned, it is very seldom that two or three of us are in the same location on a golf course. Surfing wasn't a problem as we were a three-and-a-half-hour drive from the nearest wave. So, it was with a heavy heart that we obeyed the rules, as much as possible that is, and stayed inside and did what our Government wanted.

Now how do I amuse myself being locked up in quarantine in beautiful Bright? Before I go into this, at the beginning of the COVID-19 pandemic, my wife and I followed the other six million-odd members of our great country and thought we should make an appointment to have a COVID-19 test. Big mistake. Since all this has happened, just about everyone I come across in Bright, I ask them, "have you had the COVID-19 test?" The general reply, "of course not, we're not sick so why bother."

If we had heeded that line of thinking, we would not have been tortured by the lovely nurse at the Bright Hospital. Our appointment was made and off we went. All smiles as we went in and registered that we were doing our thing for Queen and country.

My wife went in first and didn't seem to be in the adjoining room for awfully long. As she came out, she looked me in the eye and said, "you're going to enjoy this." I had seen those images on the nightly news of people in Melbourne sitting in their vehicles having the test. A simple procedure according to the images. A person, supposedly qualified to do the test, makes their way to the victim sitting quietly in the front seat of their vehicle. Then the victim puts their head back and the smiling nurse or whoever sticks a stick in the victim's mouth. What is never shown is the next part of the test. Using the same stick, both nostrils are invaded to the point of stage five torture. I am sure if this were shown on a regular basis, not a single person would volunteer for this procedure.

So, in I went. "Hi Mandy, is this going to hurt?" I asked with a hint worry in my voice. "I'll try to be as quick as possible, Graham." With those words of confidence, I sat down, put my head back and waited. But not for long, the stick went to the back of my throat, and that wasn't too unpleasant but then the real action began. "Jesus," I uttered as she then proceeded to push the stick thing up one nostril and then the other. It went so far up and then the bloody thing was twisted. I thought for a moment that each of my eyes had been pulled out of their sockets. As soon as it was done, it was over. "Would you like a chocolate on your way out, Graham?" 'A chocolate,' I thought to myself, 'bugger that, I'm going straight to the nearest solicitor to sue someone, or maybe the Human Rights Commission to lodge a claim of torture in Bright.'

After having regained some form of composure, I thanked Mandy, and wished her well in her future torturing of other locals. Back home and back to the safety and sanctuary where it was time to decide how to endure our lockdown.

Chapter 29

Whether it was good luck or a stroke of, 'I need to do something creative,' a model boat I had previously ordered arrived in the mail. It was shortly after my father's death that I was asked if I would like one of his wooden models he had built years before. Either I was turning into my father, as they say you do, or I was desperate to build something. It was the latter and the box had arrived.

First thing, where to build the bloody boat. I managed to find an old metal table and then find a spot in 'my' room. I have found that as we, well, as I get a bit older, it's comforting to have somewhere to do your own thing.

The parcel arrived in the mail, and there it was. The 'Jolie Brise.' The box was saying that the company was located in Spain, but the numerous bits-and-pieces were rounded up and packaged in Hong Kong. I opened the box to see what I was in for. Having not built anything of this nature before I was intrigued to see what all the fuss was about. All the wooden pieces seemed to be laser-cut and accompanying those bits were the sails, and literally hundreds of tiny nails and other assorted bits-and-pieces that would complete the model. I immediately thought to myself, 'how many of you lot will still be sitting in the bottom of the plastic tray when the boat is complete?'

And so, the process began. 'Follow the instructions this time, you dick head,' I said to myself. I suspect that most, if not all males, have a few too many screws, nails and, in this case, tiny pieces of model ship bits left over when constructing the latest project. I for one always seem to have at least a few screws left over when putting one of those 'flat pack' cupboards or shelves together. What to do with all these bits-and-pieces? They, of course, are left at the bottom of the third drawer in the kitchen.

"Why do you keep all those things?" my wife invariably asks. "Well, you never know when something falls out or off, then I'll have a spare piece to fix it." "Don't be stupid, you know you'll never get around to that, so just throw it away," she states, and mostly she is correct. Back to the task at hand. 'God, where do I start?' as I looked at all the full-size instructions and all those bits of laser-cut wood and accessories?

'One small step for mankind,' I think I'd heard that somewhere before, but wait, I needed a few new tools. As I made my way up to the local hardware store in Bright, I carefully considered what was required for the project. Glue, of course, something strong and sticky, a set of small pliers, and a couple of clamps. I was convinced that the clamps would be essential. I had managed to locate my old trusty hammer, so a new one wasn't required.

Back home, everything was ready. After glancing over the instructions, glue in hand and, of course, it was my favourite from 1960s. 'Tarzan's Grip.' The stuff that sticks to everything including your fingers, clothes and especially wood for model ships.

After having a quick read of the instructions and an even shorter glance at the colour diagram, I was off and sticking bits-and-pieces together like there was no tomorrow. After an hour or so, the hull was beginning to appear like one of those upturned Greek shipwrecks. Enough was enough, it was time to have a break. I glanced at the clock on the wall and noticed to my surprise that almost two hours had elapsed. I was beginning to actually enjoy the whole process, and smiled to myself, one of those smiles that no one else would notice or care about. I'll digress for a moment as there is something I need to share with you before the boat-building continues.

The Victorian Government decided to ease a few of the stricter restrictions on regional Victorians. Common sense prevailed and all of us out in regional Victoria were given the liberty to have a fishing expedition, go surfing and, most important of all as far as I was concerned, was the opportunity to play golf.

The wearing of masks was not yet mandatory, so it was time to challenge both the Bright Golf Course and my natural ability. Maskless and, for the first time in a couple of months, I may my way onto the first tee. Things were going well, I managed not to belt my ball over the fence and onto the road. Was this going to be one of 'those days?' Numerous pars, brilliant golf and a win at the end of the competition? Of course not. I made my way along the first fairway following the Srixon 3 with the black dot to the edge of the green. Without taking too much notice, as I was convinced my ball was quietly resting on the edge of the green, I walked up, putted 'my' ball towards the flag. Doing the right thing, I placed 'my' ball marker onto the green and then proceeded to wipe my ball on my shirt sleeve.

At this point in the game, all I needed to do was have a maximum of two more putts and I would have been happy. A solid six shots, two stableford points and then onto the second hole. It was when I went to replace my Srixon 3 back onto the green that I noticed that there was a spot of green moss stuck to my ball. With due diligence, I stuck my ball onto my tongue and proceeded to flick off the offending green bit. Would the green spot come off? Of course not. It immediately became obvious that I had putted some other player's ball and not my own. The only noble and correct thing to do was to own up to my stupid error and ask, "by any chance, is someone using a Srixon 3 with a bloody green dot on it?"

Our president of the golf club who is in our group explained, "thanks, Graham, oh, that's my ball, I wondered where it got to, didn't I tell you which ball I was using?" "Great, thanks for nothing, you bastard," I said to myself. It was at that point on the first green that I thought, 'it's going to be an exceptionally long day.' Wrong ball, first hole, no score, and I really shouldn't be here. Not being one to give up, but I was close, I wandered off to the second tee, but this time I changed balls and thought, 'maybe this Titleist 4 would be harder to confuse with the other three players in the group.'

To cut a long story a little shorter, the second hole was almost as bad, but at least this time I did manage to have six hits including three putts on the green. "Oh well, back to normal," I muttered to myself. The third hole at Bright Golf Club is one of those holes that looks easy. One hundred and fifty-odd metres, straight as a dye, with a small hollow on the front right-hand side. Nothing on the left apart from a row of gum trees with a couple of holiday houses overlooking the green.

Thinking, 'bugger this, I should try a bit harder this time and keep my bloody head down.' So, there I stood, head down, my five iron in hand, "shit," I said to myself quietly, "let's try something different." I placed my five iron twice the space behind the ball that I usually do when trying to get the ball in the air. A short glace to my left to see where the flag was just in case things went according to my plan.

The flag on this occasion was yellow and near the front right-hand side of the green. Yellow means the flag should be in the front third of the green. But, being realistic, and having my level of skill, it really didn't matter at all. 'Please golf god, let me firstly hit the bloody thing and, secondly, don't hook the ball to the left and end up on someone's front porch.' And it went like this.

We all understand the times when something we do like falling over or being hit by a low-lying branch, the entire process is like watching the event unfold in slow-motion. Nothing could stop the inevitable from happening. My five iron took on a life of its own. I was concentrating like there was no tomorrow, as I believed that helped the weekend hacker achieve his moment in time. I instantly thought, as the ball soared into the air, 'well, at least the ball could be heading towards the green.'

Our group of four included our president, Peter Malkin, our past club captain, Peter McGrath, who, in an earlier time, was a golf professional and, when time permitted, played the Australian Pro circuit, and Mark Frost, or as he prefers, 'Frosty.' Frosty was in the Australian army for over ten years in an earlier career. He, at the time of this major event, was the local team leader for Ambulance Victoria, and an all-round good bloke.

Sorry, I was digressing a little. Back to the flight of my Titleist 4. As the ball hit the front left of the green, it altered course slightly due to the slope of the green and began rolling to the right. The closer it got the hole the better it began to look. To my amazement, and to the others in the group standing behind me, the unthinkable was about to occur. I had been recently given the-all clear by our local optometrist that my long vision was excellent, but even I could see my ball had fallen into the hole. With the COVID-19 restrictions on the golf course, all the holes had circular pieces of foam wedged around the flags. This apparently was to prevent golfers from shoving their hands in to retrieve their ball and possibly spreading the virus.

As I pondered, Frosty grabbed his 'range finder' and held it up to his eye, and said, "yep, it's in the hole, well done." And with that, I was off in a flash towards the green. Not having experienced the elation of a hole-in-one before, and it was probably never going to happen again, I didn't know what to do. Did I jump around madly, yell and swear like I have seen others do, or what?

Talk about an anti-climax. No crowds cheering, just a couple of 'well done' but no hand-shaking or kissing. COVID-19 times will do that. I picked my ball up and carefully shoved it into my bag, so that at least it would be presented to me later accompanied by a bottle of Johnnie Walker

Scotch Whiskey. 'So that is what all the fuss is about,' I said to myself as I made my way to the fourth tee to continue on as if nothing had happened.

The rest of the round was not one to remember, more adventures into the trees, and foraging around in the long grass looking for other's balls., I did attempt to 'shout the bar' as the tradition dictates, but there was hardly another golfer left as the bar was closed due to the COVID-19 restrictions.

Oh, well, at least my wife and the rest of my family were impressed when the news was out. The funny thing about all this was, although it is exceedingly rare for a weekend golfer to achieve the ultimate, a hole-in-one. but, would you believe it, it happened to me again three weeks later, on a quiet Monday morning in the Veteran's competition! Same hole, different people, and a different golf club. This time a six iron as the tee was a bit shorter but the result was the same. Same setup, same prayer to the golf god and up and in it went. To say others were amazed would have been an understatement. So, this was the culmination of so many years wandering around aimlessly chasing a golf ball that didn't need to belong to me for more than nine holes. Each time I sit in 'my' room at home surrounded by the flotsam and jetsam of my life's collecting they are. Two cheap gold-plated plastic trophies with my two lucky golf balls stuck in, reminding me of those two times, with my name and details of the event, sitting up on a shelf collecting dust. I can only presume that they will one day end up at the tip with other discarded relics of my time on this earth.

Chapter 30

Enough of this self-reflective rubbish, it's time to get back to the story. The COVID-19 times were wearing a bit thin in our household. No travel, no visiting others and not much fun at all. I took the opportunity to, 'build another boat.' This time something larger and more complicated than my first build.

Although my first model boat construction was satisfying to say the least, something was missing. So, I scanned through the online possibilities and stumbled upon, the, wait for it, The Pen Duick. Twice the size and twice as high as my first model. I waited with increasing frustration for my package to arrive in the mail. And one day, there it was. It looked the same as on the web site, but when opened, I thought, 'my god, there is no way all these tiny pieces will be used.' For starters, five hundred and fifty tiny brass nails. Enough thin timber pieces to construct a small Ark and sails so large it seemed ridiculous.

The instructions were in book form, and colour to boot. The previous model entailed reading one large double-sided sheet, in numbered fashion and a full-size sheet explaining the mast and sail placement. So easy to read when stuck on the wall in front of me. This one, totally different. Almost a book, plus the full-size mast and sail diagram. 'My god, this will be exciting,' I muttered again to myself.

And then I began. A quick scan of the instructions, not too long a read, as I had already considered myself as an old hand in the boat building business. Bits of thin laser-cut timber lengths found a home along other lost pieces. After several hours of toil, the hull was ready for the first sand and a bit of paint. But first I have a bit of a brain-wave. 'Why don't I glue an old Australian coin in the hull as a memento of my time building the yacht?' From my bottle of old Australian pre-decimal coins, one was selected, a 1923 half-penny. It looked in good condition and at least someone in the future might come across my hidden treasure. So, in it went, and then back to the work at hand.

It was at that time the impressive shape could be seen in all its glory. The next part of the operation was to find a colour that matched the cover of the box. Black, white, and green, and still having a few pots of enamel paint left over from my signwriting days, they suited the job perfectly. After this was all dry and looking good, my attention was on all those tiny bits-and-pieces that cover the deck, you know, hatches, pulleys and other assorted things that should be on the deck of a model boat.

As I was taking a break, something in the back of my mind clicked and said, 'hey, you, wasn't there something about the 1923 Australian half-penny that rings a bell?' Onto good old Doctor Google and typed in the 1923 half-penny. Woah, I couldn't believe what I was reading. For some reason, coins of that year can be worth thousands of dollars. "Shit, you've got to be joking," I said to myself. There was only one thing to do, and that was slice the side of the yacht hull and check to see the true date on the coin.

All my hard work, pushing all those tiny nails into the ribs of the hull, endless sanding and filing of the nail heads back to a smooth surface. In two swift actions, a section approximately five centimetres wide and high was carved into where I thought the now valuable coin was hiding. With a tiny torch, I peered into the gloom only to discover that my 1923 Australian half-penny, was in fact, dated 1932.

Should I tell my wife of this boat-building error, or just not bother? There was the possibility that she could stumble into my room and see me hastily trying to rebuild the side of the yacht's hull, and then I would have to explain how my now ship-wrecked yacht needed vital repairs for its maiden voyage. I came clean, wandered into her sewing room, and explained my predicament. She looked up, laughed, and went back to what she was doing.

With the hole repaired, resanded, nails filed back, it was time to repaint the whole thing. It now sits proudly alongside the first masterpiece, the Jolie Brise. One thing that still surprises me was the vast amount of bits-and-pieces left over from both the model kits. 'Oh, well, I'll find something to do with all these leftovers,' I thought.

Chapter 31

At the time of writing this, our COVID-19 world is beginning to open again. Although we were under reasonably strict restrictions, being in regional Victoria we did take a lot for granted. Compared to the Melbourne Metropolitan area, our restrictions were nothing like those millions working from home and confined to their houses. In late November 2020, the Victorian Government opened the gates, well, the media and the Government named it, 'The Ring of Steel'. Bright was almost back to normal. The active cases of the virus had been reduced to zero and it seemed millions of Melbournians fled to greener pastures, especially to the country.

What did we do on that first weekend of freedom? We drove over the mountains and sought the relative sanctuary of Paynesville? A few hours later after leaving Bright, as if by magic, the roller door opened, and we drove into our garage and to the solace that we needed. Away from the maddening crowds, and the demands of family life.

Paynesville is one of those places that should be thriving, as I have said previously. On this return trip, after the serious lockdown that all of Victoria had been placed under, nothing much had changed. The shops and businesses bumped along to the beat of a different drummer. I recall that odd term from our travels to Dunk Island in far north tropical Queensland. The similarities are such that, apart from the climate, the locals' attitude is a little similar.

Although Dunk Island was almost destroyed by a couple of cyclones and, at the time of writing this, is still waiting for a cashed-up developer to restore the resort to its former glory. Paynesville, on the other hand, seems to be happy to be left alone by others. Sometimes busy on the weekends but generally just one of those sleepy seaside places that are happy in their own old-pleated tartan skirts and frilly-necked shirts, and that's the men. (Only joking). The retired male of the species down Paynesville way, either it's my wild imagination or it really does happen, all have the idea in their heads that they should look like Ernest Hemingway. Slightly longer hair than usual for men in their 70s. White, neatly trimmed beard, no shoes or socks, only a pair of old, well-worn sandals or thongs. The overall look is completed with a pair of old scruffy shorts and a tee shirt with the logo of one of Australia's surfing brands. Sunglasses are invariably glued to the top of their old baseball caps. I do suspect all is not what it seems, but who am I to judge?

I was waiting to take the Raymond Island ferry to whisk me over to the island one afternoon. I struck up a conversation with one of those types. He had the appearance of being retired, happily married, and comfortable with his lot. "Afternoon, it's good to be alive," were his first words. Not one to leave a conversation like that, I asked him, "do you live on the island?"

"Yes, I've been here a little over a year or so, I brought my place one day without telling my wife." "And what was her response, did she like her new home?" I asked. "Well, no, she left me, and I haven't seen her since, but I really don't care. I don't need to drive my car except to go into Bairnsdale every couple of weeks, I just ride my old bike over to the shops after getting off the ferry. I can see my boat from my house, so what more could I ask for?"

And with that, he said, "if you ever need a chat, come over and see me and we'll have a cuppa." He gave me his address and, you never know, I may call in on him one day.

Paynesville is known as the 'boating capital of Victoria' but its other claim to fame is the size of the mozzies. People we know in Bright can only recall one thing. It's not the beauty of the Gippsland Lakes, the serenity of the local 'Spinner Dolphins' cruising around in front of the local jetties, or the sight of dozens of yachts sailing on Lake Victoria, it's the size of the bloody mosquitos!

At our little humble getaway, the first and most important thing to do when arriving is to light the mozzie coils, usually, two new ones near the rear door, switch on the mozzie zapper, and then spray all the surrounding greenery with a spray that easily could kill an elephant. Only then can we try to sit outside and enjoy the serenity. Frequently, five minutes are enough and then head back inside, out of harm's way. Our friends who have visited Paynesville in the past, have described the local mozzies as big as sparrows. One friend, in particular, has described the mosquitos as the only place in the world where he has seen them swarming like a massive migration of Italian Geese.

Chapter 32

With the release of the rather arduous COVID-19 well and truly only a short memory away, it was time to clean off the cobwebs of our caravan and head for the coast. Having checked that all was well in Paynesville, our oldest son suggested, "hey, Dad, isn't it time that you and mum took the van away for a short trip? How about Barwon Heads, and we'll come too for a few days?" And with that, we booked a week 'down on the coast.' What on earth could possibly go wrong this time?

With the benefit of hindsight, not really much, as we had driven down there twice before, and keeping within the speed limit, the trip should take around four-and-a-half to five hours. As the caravan had been under cover for the past ten months due to Victorians being confined to barracks, or so it seemed, there were a couple of things that needed attending to.

The caravan manufacturer, for some to think these things are a good idea, decided that the Jayco Journey ensuite would be enhanced with a bowl more suited to planting a few succulents in. On our first trip eighteen months back in the new van, it was patently obvious that more space would be available if the bloody bowl wasn't there.

To give you an idea of what I am talking about, the overall size of our en-suite would be 2200mm x 1000mm, and in that is a toilet, toilet roll holder, a single row of tiny cupboards on the rear wall. Then the masterpiece of interior design, a vanity cupboard with two doors, and sitting proudly on top is a curved porcelain bowl 500mmx350mm and 150mm high. More about that in a moment. To the right of that vanity unit is the enclosed shower cubicle.

Back to the bowl. Sitting proudly, and I mean that literally, was the bowl. Taking into consideration that a skinny, if not anorexic person would have difficulty in drying themselves in such a confined and restricted area. The idea of a bowl leaping off the top of the vanity unit and protruding into one's stomach or backside at the slightest opportunity was cause for great concern. Maybe if we had been forty-odd years younger but being in our mid-60s, life didn't need to have some white, cold porcelain object prodding you when you least expected it.

We, or should I say, my wife found a new, and rather small vanity bowl online and, within a week, it arrived. "I'll have a go and see if I can remove the existing bowl, unscrew a few things and attach the new one, it shouldn't take too long," I said to my wife.

'Famous last words,' spring to mind. The caravan cover was still over the van, so when I bravely went where no man had been for a while, at least ten months, and armed with an arsenal of tools that I thought might have been of use. The first task was to try and unscrew the plastic pipe that was attached to the base of the old bowl. Impossible or so it seemed. Either the sink was installed by a person the size of an elf, or there had to be another way to get access. Deciding that, rather than have a breakdown and throw a tantrum on the floor, I gave an expert look to see what was what.

At first, I didn't notice a veneered panel stuck on the front of the vanity cupboard. So, with a bit of trepidation, I jammed my flathead screwdriver into the slightest of spaces. 'Maybe a bit of a belt with the hammer, and all will be revealed,' I thought to myself. No matter how hard I tried, the front panel and the cupboard were not going to part ways. Well, there had to be a way to remove the bloody thing. I probed the inside and, to my surprise, there were three screws, fixed from the inside. Obviously screwed in prior to the whole thing fitting into place.

Enough was enough. It was now or never, in went the screwdriver, a slight tap with the hammer and off the front panel came. The screws were still firmly in place, but with three new holes in the front panel. "Hopefully, it will be covered up if I ever manage to put the bloody thing back in place," I muttered to no one in particular.

I again shoved my hand back into the space holding the plastic pipe and other bits-and-pieces to see if I could unscrew anything at all. No movement, just a stubborn hard, plastic pipe where it had always been.

There was nothing to do but accept defeat, go back inside and call for a plumber. There had been a bit of an issue in the bathroom. Well, as far as my wife was concerned. Two new taps that had been installed a couple of years ago, were as stiff as an old bit of welding. I managed to endure this mild inconvenience, but my better half was at breaking point. The problem was, apart from the stiffness of the two taps, the water pressure resembled the last drops flowing out of one of those plastic wine casks. You know there is a bit more, but it just wouldn't come out.

Our new plumber was called, and to our amazement, he turned up as he said he would. No small feat for a plumber in our small country town. A quick visit out to the van and then he disappeared. It appeared ne needed a few things from the local hardware store. "Back soon." When he returned, it was back into the van and, in no time at all, the old pipes and fittings were replaced with the new basin and the water was switched back on. To my surprise he had even managed somehow to re-affix the front cover board and then wandered off to our bathroom problem.

He entered the bathroom, switched on both the taps, turned them off and said nothing. Down on the floor, he opened the front doors of the vanity cupboard, shuffled a few of those things around that really have no right to be there, and turned both the hot and cold water control taps on a bit, and bingo. When he managed to get off the floor, a quick turn of the taps on the sink and there was our lost and elusive water. It came out with such force both my wife and I couldn't believe how stupid we, well, really, I had been, not to have noticed the bloody taps inside the cupboard. In my defence, I cannot be the only male in the world not to have noticed all the accumulated, half-empty, long-forgotten makeup bags and other assorted stuff that inhabited the dark recess.

Thankfully, our plumber had the sense not to mention all 'the stuff,' but said, "I'll be back with a couple of new ones, and all should be fine." 'Fantastic,' I thought to myself, 'no more complaints from my wife.'

With those tasks completed, it was time to prepare for our trip down to Melbourne and onto Barwon Heads for a week before Christmas. Our caravan had not been taken away for close to ten months. With the year being consumed by COVID-19 lockdowns, our caravan required a bit of preparation prior to the escape to the coast.

The first thing was to check inside for spiders, long-lost clothing from our last few nights away due to the earlier bushfires. A couple of odd socks were found jammed down the back of the bedside cupboards, and my wife located a pair of earrings that she had sworn were lost.

As with a lot of things that I must deal with regarding our caravan, the first and most important thing is to attach the caravan to our tow vehicle. Although I really detest the term, 'tow vehicle,' it's what it is. According to the dozens of caravan magazines stored throughout our house, those whose lives revolve around 'their van,' the car, or four-wheel drive, is never referred to simply as that. It's always, 'the tow vehicle.'

Whether it's me, or not, that terminology just doesn't seem right, so we, my wife and I, simply call it the Ford. Anyhow, the gates were unlocked, the Ford reversed into position, and I jumped out to see how well I had done with the reversing, and immediately thought to myself, 'you've got to be joking.' The problem was, when our local council, the Alpine Shire, had the thought that after twenty-nine years of our time living at 21 Delany Avenue, it was time to pave the gravel footpath. Not so much as pave it but install a smooth tarmac two-metre-wide strip of tar that would become the latest venue for all with bikes, scooters, runners and kids being dragged along to the local swimming pool in the river.

And what is the problem with that, I hear you say? Well, the fact that the new runway/footpath was laid a good twenty centimetres above the previous gravel meant that there was no way possible that I could connect our caravan connection to the vehicle. I had just wound the four caravan supports up into their cubby hole under the van and then tried to jack up the towing assembly in front of the van. My new and wonderful hydraulic jack mechanism was performing as it should, but no matter how much I levered there was no way that the tow ball on the Ford would reach the fitting on the front of the caravan draw bar. Just one more push with the lever should do the trick, or so I thought. At this time in the manoeuvring, I had a look at the van and, from my limited knowledge about these things, the van looked like it was at a thirty-degree angle. The rear of the van was preciously one-hundred-and-fifty millimetres from our bedroom window. Suddenly! Without warning there occurred a crash that could have been mistaken for an earth tremor had I not been there to witness what had just happened.

The caravan, our pride and joy, had broken the jack with the increased pressure and landed onto the gravel below. The noise was so loud that our neighbour, Bob, raced over to see what all the fuss was about. "No problems, Bob, just a minor technical issue," I muttered to myself. Bob in his quiet nature said, "Graham, I think you need a block of wood under the jack to take the pressure off your jack." With those words of wisdom, he vanished back into his workshop and shortly returned with a couple of bits of wood that he considered right for the task.

The first task was to remove my jack that was now lying in the gravel under the drawbar of the van. Extraction would have been a more suitable term, but there was just enough space to lever it out. A block of wood was placed into position and the process began again. This time under the careful supervision of Bob.

Slowly but surely, the caravan began to rise, further and further, until it was just possible to reverse the Ford back into position once again. All the while my wife was oblivious to what was taking place in her front garden.

The idea was that when we finally drove the van out of its little cubby hole, I would drive across the road and park on the other side while my wife would then drive her vehicle into the spot where the caravan had been for the past ten months and shut the double gates. Now, this sounds reasonably simple. The idea when travelling anywhere in our caravan, is you depart early and arrive early at your destination.

While I was patiently sitting in the Ford over the other side of Delany Avenue, hazard lights flashing so that no one would run into me, I became a little impatient with what my wife was doing. She drove into the parking area and there she sat. Lights off, gates still open and no movement. Nothing. After what seemed an eternity, she reappeared. Slowly closed the double gates and wandered over towards my direction. At this point I had switched off the engine and began to read the newspaper. Not really but if I had one, I could have read the first half a dozen pages.

"Where on earth have you been and what have you been doing?" I asked politely, "it would be good to leave at least before we need to stop for lunch." "Well, I've just been listening to a fascinating program on the radio, you should hear it."

Words weren't necessary to ensure our next five hours of driving was going to be pleasant, I switched the engine on and drove out of Bright heading for the freeway, just an hour down the Great Alpine Road. Stan, the dog, had already been deposited at the Chiltern Hilton Kennels the previous afternoon so there was nothing to stop us enjoying our week away at the Barwon Head Caravan Park.

Close to four hundred-and-fifty kilometres is about the limit for us in one day's driving dragging our caravan behind us. A couple of stops, first, at the service centre south of Seymore to refuel and grab something for morning tea. Having invariably not taken anything in the past for these stops, this time we were ready. Having refuelled, we drove on for a hundred metres or so and parked in a truck parking bay. Squeezing in between a couple of B doubles wasn't an issue, line up, drive straight and don't deviate. From our experience, most professional truck drivers appear to tolerate caravan owners and, in most cases that we have experienced, give us a wide berth.

So, there we were, squeezed in between the trucks having our morning tea, oblivious to the outside world. How civilised all this was. A bit like playing house on a minor scale, all the while pretending those huge trucks were not next door. It wasn't long before our caravan was shaking as both the B doubles lurched off at the same time. Oh, well, at least the area for us to manoeuvre out of the truck stop was a lot easier.

Travelling down the Hume Freeway dragging our caravan is about uncomplicated as it can get. Stay in the left lane all the way to Melbourne. Then things become a lot more complicated. At the end of the Hume, the freeway becomes the Western Ring Road. This sounds a bit romantic, but it's the complete opposite. Eight lanes of traffic all trying their best to circumvent the metropolitan road network. Having driven down the Ring Road many times, but only twice before towing a caravan, we know it was best not to say a word to each other for at least the next half an hour till we reached the Geelong Freeway. Driving from the end of the Hume until the Geelong Freeway, I knew that there would be two lane changes for the duration. That was not going to happen on this occasion. Trucks, cars, taxis were all hurtling west with us all finding the need to cross in front, jam on their brakes and, in general, create hell for us poor 'old crackers' from the country.

Eventually, the turn off to the Geelong Freeway appeared, and at last we felt a little more comfortable with proceedings. Then it happened. "What was that noise, why is the car beeping at us?" my wife exclaimed as she does at the most inopportune moment. "Don't worry, it's only the bloody car telling us that we need put some of the bloody Ad-blue in the tank." "Should we stop at the next service centre and fill it up?" she said. "No, it'll be right until we get to Barwon Heads, and I'll fill it up tomorrow."

Dealing with the constant stream of traffic and the cars constantly beeping at me, things suddenly became noticeably quiet in our car. "There, pull in at the next bend at the service centre on the Geelong Bypass, I can't stand the strain any longer, what happens if the car stops right now, what are we going to do?"

Rather than continue in silence, common sense prevailed and in we went. To my surprise this particular service centre was one of the largest ones we had come across. I noticed the Ad-blue on one of the bowsers and headed straight for it. Fortunately, there were two fittings on the nozzle, one for trucks and the other for frazzled caravan owners. Having come across one of these way out in the middle of outback Queensland, even with my knowledge of these things, I knew it was going to be a good end. Nozzle straight in, ten dollars paid, and we were back onto the Geelong Bypass.

Conversation was flowing, things were good. "Aren't you glad we filled up and wasn't it a good idea of mine?" Words weren't necessary, as we made our way south. Having been down to Torquay and Barwon Heads many times over the years, but only twice before dragging the van I thought I knew the way. One small turn-off to the left and follow the signs to our destination, Barwon Heads. When writing this, I immediately thought of the Australian film, The Castle. 'We're off to Bonnie Doon,' the place where you can really 'feel the serenity.'

Anyhow, to cut a long story a bit shorter, I took one turn to the left too early. From what should have been a quite easy drive from the turn-off from the freeway turned out to be the complete opposite. Somehow we found ourselves driving past the new area known as Armstrong's Creek, an entirely new housing development. When we had finally regained some form of direction, we turned right onto the main Torquay Road.

It seemed that every five hundred metres or so there was a set of traffic lights to contend with. Silence again as we slowly tried to anticipate all the other hundreds of vehicles that were trying to make our drive hell.

After what seemed like an eternity, the turn-off to Barwon Heads appeared on the brow of a hill. Thankfully, several years ago, the once dangerous intersection had been reconfigured into one of those wonderful roundabouts. A slow down, give way to the right, where we should have been half an hour ago and we were on the home-stretch. After five hours of dodging all types of traffic, there up the road in front of us was a series of roads that could have been a match for the Western Ring Road.

There is always something about those signs that creep up on you when roadworks appear in the distance. You know the ones, a smallish sign depicting a man with a shovel and a pile of dirt at his feet. I am sure that in our times of political correctness, there will be a male and a female each holding a shovel and looking away from the other, each waving their shovel at the oncoming traffic.

There was ours, up in the distance, preceded by dozens of stationary vehicles all in a 'conga line.' Giving myself enough distance in front so as not to collide with my nearest opponent up in front, we gradually made our way to the back of the queue. Two weeks before Christmas to our thinking didn't seem to be the right time to undertake these massive resealing works. But really, is there ever a good time to do these, I suppose not?

Another twenty minutes later we entered the outskirts of Barwon Heads. Thankfully, several years ago the main access through the town and onto Ocean Grove had been diverted away from the main street, Hitchcock Avenue. A short drive and the turn-off to the Barwon Heads Caravan Park. The entrance is a little obscured on the right. Just before the bridge over the Barwon River.

For those who can remember, a couple of decades back, there was an Australian television series named 'Sea Change.' Set in a fictitious seaside town, the series was immensely popular with audiences both in Australia and overseas. Barwon Heads had always been a popular holiday destination for families. Always popular over the Christmas and Easter holiday times, but generally went to sleep for the rest of the year. The main place to stay was the Barwon Heads Caravan and Camping Park.

With 'Sea Change' being produced and aired, the town experienced an overnight explosion in popularity. Gone were the quaint shops providing the locals with their daily needs and requirements, to be replaced with a plethora of clothing shops, cafés, and real estate agent businesses. More about that shortly.

We made our way to the area at the entrance to the caravan park, I jumped out, well, really hobbled out of the Ford after sitting in the same seat for over five hours and went to check-in. We had been delighted that our oldest son, Andrew, his wife, Daisy, and their two children had chosen to spend a few nights in their new caravan in the same park.

As I was paying for the week, I mentioned that our family was also staying and would also be arriving at the same time. "Oh, Mr Badrock, they have already checked in a day earlier." For as long as I can recall, our family, the Badrocks, have never arrived early for trips away, but often have the propensity to leave at least a day earlier than their booking. Anyhow, although Andrew and his family live in Bright, we don't seem to live in each other's pockets – it would be good to catch up with them.

The phone rang. "Where are you? Let us know when you arrive, and I'll help you reverse into your site." "Hi, Andrew, funny you should call, we are making our way down the road to our site now, see you shortly."

We had been given a map when we checked in and, with my limited computer skills, I already had some idea of where we should be going. As we made our way down the main access drive, past the football oval and left onto the second track, past the amenities block, and there on the left was our site for the next seven nights. Site Number 146. Having stayed in the caravan park twice before in recent years, we knew that being exposed to the elements, a site directly beside the Barwon River, was scenic, but prone to being blown off the land and into the water.

The site we chose, one of the few remaining, when we booked did appear to offer some protection from the weather. Just two sites from the river, our allotted site was nestled beside a large and bulky line of tea-trees. When we finally made it, I couldn't believe it. There was a car parked, on 'our' site. No one around, not a soul, let alone the owner. At that instant, as I was about to phone the reception, our son, Andrew, appeared and took charge of the situation. "Don't worry, the owner is sure to return shortly." 'As if that was going to happen,' I thought to myself.

As if by a miracle just as I was thinking, 'what's next,' the owner of the car returned. "Sorry, mate, just trying to keep my car out of the sun." At least he was polite, but the thought of me complaining to a tattoo-covered man, over six foot in the old term and wearing a singlet and a pair of torn shorts, was quickly washed out of my now-frazzled brain.

I drove forward and then attempted to reverse onto the site. If I can explain the situation this way, it might help to give you some understanding of my predicament. Off to the left in front of us was a light post. You know the type, the one that jumps out in front of you when you least expect it. Immediately on my right was an impenetrable row of thick native tea-trees. My target was a narrow section of ground immediately behind our caravan.

After several, futile attempts to reverse onto the site, our eldest son took control. As they sometimes feel the need to do so. "Drive forward, right hand down." "Why do I need to put my right hand down?" I cheekily replied. "Just do as I suggest and all will be good," he said. Eventually, both the caravan and the Ford were heading in the right direction. "That'll do," I replied.

And with that, our home-away-from-home was tucked up beside the Barwon River. The unpacking and setting up of the van were certainly a lot easier than reversing onto the site. There was one good thing to come out of all this, we were only one hundred metres from our son's caravan. Not too close, but close enough, if you understand what I am saying.

The weather forecast was for a couple of warm sunny days, then the weather could change. We know from experience that in Victoria, there really can be four seasons in one day. Would that be the case? We'll have to wait and see.

Barwon Heads is quite a different place in recent times. Over the next couple of days our wanderings took us to familiar landmarks, The Bluff, the back beach, and the iconic jetty. Now the jetty is a location that allows both the tourists and locals to pretend that there is a possibility they may catch a fish or two. Being the eternal optimist, it wasn't long before we headed down the path back to the jetty. Rods, hooks, sinkers, bait, and my old fishing basket, which doubled as a seat. 'We' need a seat when sitting on a jetty for a couple of hours especially when sixty-seven years are looming in the birthday world.

Tides are things that have always intrigued me. I sort of understand the concept of the earth and the moon thing creating the ebb-and-flow of the oceans, but the difference in water height has me stumped. So, there we were, baiting up, casting off into the Barwon River and immediately seeing our fishing lines sucked towards the Barwon River Bridge. This accompanied by huge volumes of seaweed passing in front of where we were sitting all heading in the same direction. The seaweed had the look of King Neptune's hair having been torn off to frustrate our small fishing group. No sooner had our line and hook hit the water and the entire cluster of hooks, lines, sinker, and bait were being dragged unceremoniously towards the bridge. If anyone had noticed our small group, it could have been like, 'wow, I wonder what's on their line?' They would have been immediately disappointed as we were, when trying to drag a large clump of seaweed back to the jetty.

To my complete amazement, I managed to catch a couple of suicidal fish. A couple of ridiculously small whiting and an even smaller mullet. At least my grandson, Banjo, was impressed, while his father stated, "you call that a fish, it's more like a bit of bait." "And how many have you caught, Andrew? I muttered under my breath.

After an hour of having been snagged numerous times by the endless stream of seaweed, it was time to pack up and return to the camp site. "Just one more, Popo," said Banjo. It you ever are in the position of having your only- grandson ask that question, it goes without saying there was no alternative but to thread another bit of bait on and continue feeding the seaweed. I noticed a man, maybe in his early forties, who appeared to be a little distracted. Maybe it was the thought he might catch a fish or two, or maybe he escaped his family for some time to himself. Anyhow, he was armed with his rod, a small tackle box and a bucket. Well, at least he was an optimistic fisherman, the bucket was a good sign. A few others were further along the jetty, all preoccupied with what they were doing. A young couple, she was interested in him, and he was interested in fishing.

As the male who had just arrived was getting ready for the afternoon's fishing, as soon as his hook, bait and sinker hit the water, his rod was almost ripped out of his hands. Suddenly the chatter that was coming from all of us ceased immediately. All eyes were on our champion fisherman. Whatever it was, and it wasn't a lump of seaweed, was doing its utmost not to come out of the water.

After what seemed to be an inordinate amount of time, I suspect it was no longer than a minute, but time did seem to stand still, and the monster from the deep broke the surface. Gasps could be heard and kids on the jetty raced over to see what all the fuss was about. I noticed even those dining in the restaurant at the beginning of the jetty had seen what was unfolding and stood up and stared.

His fishing rod was bent over so much that I really thought it might break. With one last heave of his rod, the fish was flung out of the water and onto the worn timber decking. Flapping around like there was no tomorrow, it was no match for our hero fisherman. He grabbed his bucket, asked one of the kids to make sure his fish didn't flop back into the water, and raced back along the jetty, down the steps and into the water below. Bucket filled with seawater, and in a flash, he was back. Quickly the monster silver trevally was shoved in headfirst, with the tail sticking out of the top.

After the excitement had calmed down, I casually sauntered over, I had to mask my excitement somehow and asked him about his fishing exploits.

"So, do you come here often, and is this the normal size you are targeting?" "No mate, this is the first time in twenty-five years I have been fishing here, I used to fish here as a kid, I'm just as surprised as everyone else." And with that he packed up and departed. I was sure that his family would be regaled with all the details of his return to the Barwon Heads Jetty. Impressed I was and so were the rest of my family.

I returned a couple of days later, on my own, fish tally; two toadies and a tiny mullet. At least this time the tide was going out, no seaweed and no one else to witness my lack of fishing ability. But and there is always a but, deciding the only thing to do was prior to heading back to the campsite, was to toss all the remaining squid and prawns back into the water, and think of the monster trevally. In a perfect world, that should have been mine, haha.

After our first couple of truly delightful sunny days, the weather forecast was predicting a change. A change down at Barwon Heads can mean only one thing. Wind and rain. The only thing was to drive to the nearby Australian seaside town of Torquay. Having close relatives living in Torquay since the late-1970s, our visits have been somewhat sporadic since those early times. It seems that each time over the past four decades Torquay and the entire Surf Coast region as it's known, has experienced extraordinary growth in both population and development.

Originally a summer camping and surfing destination, Torquay has become an urban extension of nearby Geelong. According to what I could find, at the end of December 2017, the population of Torquay was close to twenty-one thousand. With recent rampant development, I would presume those figures would be pushing towards the thirty thousand mark. Gone is the small and quaint shopping centre, it's still there though, but the traffic on the day that attempted to park there was horrendous.

The old Torquay Primary School built in the 1960s had been demolished and a new primary school was built on the outskirts of the town. In its place was another, new sterile shopping complex, one of those that are found in most suburban areas throughout Australia. I suppose all those living in the area do need to be able do their shopping somewhere, but to me, it all seemed a bit chaotic. People move to these destinations, both rural and sea changers because of their locations and Bright is one of those destinations. The same I would presume as Torquay and the Surf Coast.

We, fortunately, found a car park in the new complex, and wandered around looking for things we really didn't need. I looked at my wife, "let's drive down the road to Anglesea and find a café for lunch, what do you think?" "Let's go, I can't stand this any longer, it must be quieter in Anglesea than here."

After half an hour of 'following the leader' in our convey of cars driving along the Great Ocean Road, we entered the delightful town of Anglesea. To quote 'The Iron Chef' of Japanese TV fame, 'if my memory serves me well,' the tiny town of Anglesea was just a stop off on the way to the larger town of Lorne. A small shopping strip, a pub, and a caravan park behind the beach. A surf club, a collection of fibro holiday shacks, a peddle-o boat hire on the river, and that was about it.

I must admit, we had travelled to Lorne over the past few years, but we hadn't taken the time to stop in Anglesea for any extended time. This time, stopping and, dodging the traffic was our first objective. As if by a miracle, a car parking spot became vacant and in we went. There was café after café, all trying to extract a dollar or three from the hordes of visitors who had invaded the town. One thing I did notice immediately was the local Commonwealth Bank had closed its doors. The same thing had recently happened in Barwon Heads. Was this a sign of the times, who knows?

We chose the first café that had a table free, plonked ourselves down and waited for someone to notice we were there. Shortly, a waiter presented himself, cool as a cucumber, long hair in ponytail, all black clothing, and a polite attitude to a couple of old crackers, as our adult children call us.

Morgan's Bar and Grill was rather wonderful. After pretending that we could cook for the last few days in our caravan, the thought of someone else doing the cooking, and doing the dishes was enough for us to ignore the huge volume of traffic passing fifty metres away.

A cold beer for myself and a glass of white wine for my wife ensured our lunch was one to savour for the rest of the day. I know it's a funny thing, but as we walk past those who are already sitting at their table at either a café or a restaurant, we wonder what they are thinking. As soon as my wife and I are in that position, we can sometimes be engrossed in the parade of passers-by. Commenting on their age, attitude, dress and so on. It seems there can be an invisible wall separating those sitting and those passing. I suspect we all do it, and as soon as we leave, we look around at who is sitting in 'our seats.'

Lunch was enjoyable at Morgan's Bar and Grill, but it was time to forge ahead with the rest of our afternoon. The one and only place in

Anglesea to grasp a complete view of the surrounding area was from Loveridge Lookout. I had a faded memory of this place from my days as a child when my grandfather owned a house in Lorne. The rather iconic, white structure was, according to the plaque that sits beside it, to acknowledge James Loveridge by his widow, Bertha. Constructed in 1938, it seems to be built on Art Deco lines. It has, as long as I can recall, always been painted vivid white. According to the plaque, it was James Loveridge's favourite viewing site over Bass Strait.

Over the Second World War years the lookout served as an observation post. Manned continuously between 1939 and 1945 by fifty-six local volunteers, the lookout played a critical role in the ground warning strategy of the Royal Australian Air Force. During the war years, a small room was constructed adjacent the lookout, to house a kerosene lamp and a pot belly stove. To complete the security, a barbed wire fence was constructed around both. Over three thousand aircraft were recorded during its time as an observation post, but it's not stated if any were from the enemy.

To those who are not familiar with the Loveridge Lookout, let me describe it this way. Imagine one of those incredibly old irons used to iron clothes a hundred years back. One that would be required to sit on a red-hot stove to heat up. Flat on the bottom, two pieces of steel, one on either end holding the handle. Now imagine turning the whole structure upside down, paint it white, and there you have it. According to those who know these things, it is a reinforced concrete structure, that has only recently been added to the Victorian Heritage Register. Worth a look? You bet. The views are spectacular, and it's not hard to imagine seventy-five years ago, when the Second World War had finished, what a relief it must have been to the local community members. Let alone all those others in Australia who were defending its shores.

Enough of that, one last glance back in the direction where I spent a lot of my childhood, Lorne, and it was back in the Ford for the drive back to Barwon Heads. As we were returning into Barwon Heads, I still couldn't believe the size of the growth down on the Bellarine Peninsula. Having recently looked online at the real estate listings for the town, it was staggering to think that a million dollars could buy you a shack nowhere near the beach. And that would be if you were lucky. The days when the dream of owning a beach shack for family escapes are well and truly over. That is unless you are very wealthy and have the means to do so.

When we arrived back at the caravan park, we found the number code to pass through the boom gate at the entrance, which in my case is always a worry. We looked ahead and the weather didn't look to good. The clouds had taken on the appearance of charcoal, the sea gulls seemed to be flying backwards, and the tea trees were straining to stand erect. Now doesn't that give you an idea something odd was about to occur.

Although our van was nestled behind the row of trees, the side annex was doing its best to fly off into the Barwon River. I had managed to tie everything down before we left. Numerous pegs were anchoring the awning posts into the sand, pegs had been hammered at the bottom of the side privacy screen and even a tree immediately to the left came in handy as a solid anchor. Still, the wind was reaching gale force, so I manoeuvred the Ford as close as practicable to the open side of the awning as a wind break.

My wife, at this stage, was inside the van, making herself a cup of tea, watching some program on the tv, while I was still outside fighting the elements. Trying to find some spot under the awning out of the wind and rain was becoming a bit futile. I have always enjoyed sitting outside our van reading the newspaper or even a book if I become desperate. It was when the rain turned to hail, and the hail was bouncing around inside the awning, that I simply gave up and retreated inside.

Storms don't seem to last too long down at Barwon Heads, and it wasn't long before our little world had returned to some form of normality. Walkers and runners returned as if by magic to the boardwalk beside the river. The only thing to do after all this excitement was to book in for dinner at the Barwon Heads Hotel.

It was nice to once again catch up with the rest of our family who was leaving in the morning. A bit like the Last Supper. A booking for six at six, so we all sauntered off to the pub. COVID-19 check-in, sanitize the hands, and we were in. Our last couple of meals in this iconic place were exceptional and, on this occasion, these were exactly as we had hoped. I don't know where the hotel finds all those good-looking young people behind the bar and taking our orders, but I suspect it could be from the breeding. Wealthy good-looking people usually combine to bear good-looking children, or so it seems. The ones we met were friendly, polite and a credit to their parents, no matter what their station in life was.

Our last couple of days were spent doing a bit of beachcombing along the rugged back beach. Although it was only myself and another couple of lonely beachcombers wandering west from the Bluff, my wife said, "thanks, but no thanks, there's no way I'm walking up and down the bloody stairs."

A short walk up the hill behind the caravan park will bring you to the rear entrance of the park. Although now barricaded off to keep out late-night revellers, and undesirables. The old road still provides access for those who feel the need to walk up the lookout on the top of the Bluff, or alternatively walk down those 'bloody steps' and onto the back beach. Beach could be a bit of a misnomer.

It certainly isn't a beach that anyone should think of going for a paddle or a swim. Surfers are the only brave souls who venture into the water, at least they are attached to a leg rope. There are rocks strewn for a couple of hundred metres west from the sandstone Bluff, and then the rocks give way to the ocean. An indication of how dangerous this stretch of coastline can be is the waves crashing almost directly onto the sand, and then sucking back anything still on the sand, back into the turbulent blue-green waters of Bass Strait.

On this morning, as I neared the top of the road from the caravan park, the conditions were not the most pleasant. A gale-force wind was roaring across from Bass Strait, so strong that I was sure I was about to be blown back up those 'bloody stairs.' Never one not to take the opportunity to find something, anything of interest on a wild and wind-blown stretch of sand, this morning was pushing the boundaries of my enthusiasm.

Down at the bottom of the stairs, a decision was to be made. Do I turn left and try to circumvent the Bluff or turn right and head in the direction of Thirteenth Beach? The warning signs at the bottom of the stairs seemed to shout out, 'don't attempt to walk around the Bluff in bad weather or when the tide is coming in.' Once before on our previous trip to the Barwon Heads, my wife and I did the trek. Conditions were benign, the tide was going out and the sea looked like a mill pond. Even so, there was no sunbaking on the sand, no taking selfies with the ocean in the background. Just a quick look here and there and to quote the great Australian saying, 'no rooting around.' For those who have no idea what this means, it's not having a quickie behind the rocks, it's not stopping in case the tide turns and you are caught on a rock ledge for the night.

I took heed of the warning and headed for Thirteenth Beach. How far to go, well, as far as the next set of stairs along the beach. It isn't the easiest place for a stroll, the sand was loose and fine, but still, the thirty-degree angle didn't help. The old saying, 'what goes up, must go down,' was the reverse in this instance. It appeared that the access stairs had been constructed approximately five hundred metres apart. Having found absolutely 'stuff all' on the high tide line, it was time to consider the ascent back up the cliff.

As I was about to start ambling over to the base of the stairs, a male figure appeared not far away in front of where I was heading. I am usually quite aware of my surroundings, but on this occasion, I must have been preoccupied with my beachcombing. Whether it was the noise of the pounding of the surf or the shrill of the wind, he did startle me. A person of my age, with long hair, greying beard, shorts, tee shirt and no shoes. 'My god,' I thought to myself, 'a real beachcomber.'

Ocean beaches can be strange places, places to wander alone, as I was doing, without a care in the world. Contact with others can usually be with a wave or a smile but generally not much on the conversation front. In this instance, I began to feel a little uncomfortable. He was heading in my direction, but not heading for the stairs. I managed a smile and a nod, but nothing was offered in return. Was I invisible? I thought not. He stared and looked directly at me. Not one to linger in this situation, I began the ascent up to the top of the cliffs, while he thankfully continued along the sand.

As I reached the top of the stairs, he was heading off into the distance to the base of the Bluff. What became of this encounter, nothing, but I was glad to be back on the higher part of the cliff. Was I the intruder, possibly, but how would he have known? Beaches are there to be enjoyed, but on this occasion, I wasn't convinced.

As I have mentioned in the past, the Badrocks have had a reputation for not staying the distance. I should mention that this had been the domain of my parents, Joan, and Bert Badrock. For as long as I can remember, they, for some reason, have ended their holidays at least a day early. Whether it be the weather, the company or some other trivial reason, my parents would end their travels prematurely. On one memorable occasion, they had flown halfway around the world to England for a month's travelling around the region. No sooner had they arrived at Heathrow, and they went to collect their luggage from the carousel, there was nothing to be collected. Lost in transit, I believe the term is.

My parents, then in their mid-seventies, just didn't need that. To their dismay, no record could be found, so the airline in question decided to put them up for the night at one of the airport hotels. Assuring them that everything possible was being done, they were given a small amount of cash to purchase the essential items, toothbrushes, toothpaste, and a few other things they needed. After another twenty-four hours, still no sign of their belongings. They were given another night's accommodation, returned to the hotel only to find their room had been cleaned and given to another guest.

At this stage in proceedings, they had given up all hope and demanded that they be put on the first flight back to Melbourne. From my memory, it was an exceptionally long twenty-four -flight, an extremely long twenty-four hours at Heathrow, and an excruciatingly long flight back home. This brings me to the family's reputation for cutting their holidays short. As much as my wife and I try, we have mostly managed to avoid leaving our holiday destinations. This time though there was no way we were going to or needed to endure another night in our van with the wind, rain and the occasional hailstorm tossed in for good measure.

The decision was made on our second last morning. "Let's go, at least we will be able to break Stan out of the kennels a day earlier," I said to my wife. "Great idea, start packing." Having practised this routine many times before, it didn't take too long, and we were ready to hitch up the van and drive out of the park.

The rear lights were checked, brakes, indicators and stop lights and then we were ready to drive off the site. On the immediate right-hand side of our site, there was a slight embankment, maybe only half a metre high, having started to the left to avoid this, I was aghast to see in the side revision mirror, our caravan appeared to almost fall off the embankment. I think I might have needed to reassess the situation, reverse back in, and have another go. On the spur of the moment, common sense went out the window. I slowly continued with my eyes shut for a split second. As we turned to the right, the caravan followed us in the same line.

After all this excitement, I quietly mentioned to my wife, "I almost tossed the caravan over on its side, I think we were a bit lucky this time." "You what! Don't tell, I don't want to know." And that's how we departed Barwon Heads.

The trip back home, back along the Geelong Freeway, onto the Western Ring Road and eventually the Hume Freeway, went as well as we could have hoped for. The only issue was avoiding the masses who felt the need to encircle us as we headed north. Not content to drive right behind us, but the urge to overtake at the slightest opportunity created a sense that we shouldn't have been allowed on the road. I have realised a long time ago that when towing a caravan anywhere, there isn't a need to be in a hurry. I for one didn't understand this as I too was critical of those 'old crackers' who take their vans out once or twice a year for their annual holidays. I have memories, not particularly happy, of being the last vehicle at the end of a long line of frustrated drivers, all stuck behind a caravan far ahead in the distance. Now, we, have evolved into those 'old crackers,' but when driving along a divided freeway, the world can indeed pass and travel as fast as they wish. We, on the other hand, drive within our means; one, we are not in a hurry, and two, there is always the need to conserve our fuel. It is different on a single-lane road, we do pull off to the side when safe, and let the world pass by.

As in the past when driving up the Hume Freeway, it is always necessary to refuel at least halfway home. Not willing to attempt to drive into one of the normal service centres that dot the Hume, we have found it easier to pull off and into the service centre just south of Seymore. Avoiding the area for cars and the like, it's refreshing to drive off to the left and enter the truck refuelling area.

So, there we were, quietly stationary, minding our own business, well, I was, my wife had walked over to the retail area to purchase a couple of desperately needed coffees. I was left on my own filling up the diesel in the Ford. Within a couple of minutes, our convoy of Ford and caravan was hemmed in on either side. On one side a massive B Double semi-trailer and on the other side one of those huge trucks transporting cattle. You know the type, the ones that are sometimes blocking the traffic on a country road. On this occasion there it was, right beside me. Two decks of not-happy cattle, with cascades of cattle shit running out on the side right along the Ford. To make matters worse, another truck, it too of epic proportions, had driven up behind the van. I smiled, and he gave one of those waves that indicated, 'hey, you dickhead, hurry up.' I did my best, filled the tank, went over to pay and drove off as soon as possible. One minor thing, my wife wasn't anywhere to be seen. Whether it was divine intervention or not, she suddenly appeared at the end of the car park, the northern end of the complex. "I couldn't see you among those huge trucks. I thought you might have forgotten me," she explained.

Sheepishly I muttered, "of course, I wouldn't forget you, I was just manoeuvring for a quieter location, away from the cattle truck." 'Liar, liar, pants on fire,' I thought to myself. No more was said and it was back onto the Hume Freeway and the next stop, the Chiltern Hilton to collect Stan.

Chapter 33

Christmas was just around the corner. We waited and we waited. No one else put their hand up again, so it was unanimously agreed that Christmas would be at 21 Delany Avenue. They say, 'Christmas can bring out both the good and bad in families' and this year was one of those great Christmases. All those inconvenient moments throughout the past twelve months were forgiven, and everyone managed to be polite and giving to each other. It had been agreed that the good old 'Chris Kringle' be the way to go. Everyone was to buy a generic present to the value of $50.00.

Names were drawn from a hat and each person had one opportunity to swap with the previous person's present. Of course, this was after the said present had been opened. Bottles of gin were eagerly swapped, much to the disappointment of the short-term owner. All was forgiven, well, I would think so. Lunch was an epic event. Thirteen aluminium chairs, borrowed from the Lions Club, sat glistening in the summer sun, in front of three large plastic trestle tables. All joined together in a long line and decorated by my wife. "One thing I'm sure of this year, is we, are going to have more food, last time we ran out." There was no point in even trying to have a different opinion, I just went with the flow.

So, there we all were, enjoying our Christmas in the garden, the grandchildren doing what they needed to do, the adults and parents enjoying a beer, wine and of course, the most fashionable drink at the moment, a gin and bloody tonic. Not your old standard, Gordons, Gilbey's or even a Sapphire Bombay Gin, all around the forty Australian dollar mark. But a couple of those locally-made gins, starting around eighty dollars. Someone has a lot to answer for. Boutique Australian distilleries are popping up all over Australia. And even so in Bright. One of our sons even has a collection of the local gins. Anyhow, what I was leading to was, as the lunch was proceeding under the two umbrellas and the surrounding trees, our dog, Stan, had found something in the garden. Not anywhere but almost right under one of the tables.

Our garden where we were celebrating Christmas lunch was surrounded on two sides by ivy that had gotten out of control. Stan, to his credit, I really don't know if you can credit our Stan with anything, but his attention had moved from leftover food dropped onto the ground and shifted to the ivy. Considering that Stan is totally preoccupied with anyone he comes into contact with, to see him focused on the ivy with such intensity caught everyone's attention. "Maybe it's a lizard," I said, trying to calm the situation.

Stan was, at this stage, leaning in, nose first, rear legs at a forty-five-degree angle and growling into the ivy. "Stan, come here, you stupid dog, something might bite you," I was thinking, 'This will be a bit inconvenient if I have to find a vet on Christmas day.' Something else diverted his attention away and lunch resumed, and we promptly forgot the intrusion.

We all survived another Christmas, much to our relief. There were reports of snakes on social media, 'be aware, snake on the Cherry Walk.' 'Snake on Mountbatten Avenue near the Rotary water slide,' snakes seen everywhere, or so it appeared.

I do admit that the snake that was shown, now squashed down near the Rotary water slide was a little too close for comfort. Being a little over three hundred metres from 21 Delany Avenue, there was only one thing to do. Walk around the corner and see what all the fuss was about. And there it was. Dead, still glistening in the sun and close to one and a half metres. A decent brown snake is anyone's idea of something that could kill you. A quick photo on my phone and back to tell my wife all about it.

Karen has a morbid fear of snakes, while I am more intrigued. "What! How big was it? Now I'm not going outside for the rest of this summer." "Well, at least it was dead, you do realise they can be anywhere in the countryside. Remember the huge one that had been run over outside our front gate a couple of years ago?" It didn't seem to matter she was terrified of what could be lurking in our garden. "Can we move to New Zealand, right now, they don't have any snakes?" That was the end of our conversation.

A couple of weeks later, both my wife and daughter were convinced that they had witnessed the tail of a snake disappearing into the garden right outside our back door. What to do? Do I pretend that I didn't hear anything, or be a bit more proactive? Being the responsible type that I am, something needed to be done. Put it off for a few weeks or start demolishing the whole rear garden.

My mind was made up, not through any feeling of responsibility, but the fact that our neighbour, Bob, sauntered around to our back gate, banged onto a window and beckoned me to come outside for a quick chat.

Neighbours are wonderful and in our little part of the world, we are fortunate indeed. Bob quietly mentioned, "I just thought you need to know, Graham; I have just seen a metre long brown snake in the laneway between both our houses. I managed to shoo it away from our side brick wall, but it headed straight for your fence." 'Gee thanks, Bob, for the information.' "You've got to be fucking joking," I said quietly to myself when he left.

And so, the process began. Having been in our house now for close to thirty years, the back garden had taken on a life of its own. Originally a bare open space, we decided to plant a few trees to create a bit of an oasis. Move on to recent times, and we could hardly see the tree-covered Apex Hill looming at the rear of our property. A couple of years back we employed a local contractor to remove half a dozen of the larger trees. This of course allowed the remaining vegetation, trees and shrubs to grow even faster. More light, more space, and off it all went again.

Chapter 34

For the past few years, we have enjoyed our greenery, but when the combination of jungle and snakes came into play, I knew it was time to act. Where to start? Do I begin at the back door area of the garden where the reported latest snake sighting was? Of course not. The pathway that led to the garden shed right down the back was the first to feel the sharp edge of the spade. Out came the row of carefully manicured rosemary bushes which had all reached a height of close to a metre. All following the curve of my 'crazy concrete' paving. One thing I really didn't notice until they were unceremoniously heaved out of the ground was, how much they had encroached onto the path. 'My God, look how big the bloody path is when the plants are removed,' I thought to myself. One thing I have found when tackling something as ominous as removing a large part of the garden is that you can immediately see the results of your toil.

'I suddenly had a thought.' When my wife says that I tend to run away and hide, as it usually can only mean one thing. It is going to be a lot of work and invariably takes a long time. In this instance, it was me. 'Where's my bloody trailer?' I noticed that it wasn't in its normal place down the end of our driveway. Our youngest son, Doug, is the one who borrows it. I have no problems with that, but, and there is always a but, I seem to always have to go and collect it from his home.

Doug has the best of intentions, "no worries, Dad, I'll return it as soon as I finish using it." He, his wife, Sarah, and their girls live in one of the highest locations in Bright. Of course, that location comes with steep driveways and roads. That can only mean one bloody thing. My trailer, and I do own the thing, was sitting down the end of his driveway. No one home, but his three chickens merrily clucking away at the top of his drive. The thought of walking both down and up his forty-five-degree angle drive can fill me with dread. Do I really at my age need to do this? I usually try when visiting their home to avoid this expedition. In this instance, there was no walking down, but there was the need to reverse down the cliff and stop in front of my trailer.

At the bottom of the drive, of course. is their garage. My trailer was in front of the locked door, so this presented a bit of a problem. My Ford was at the forty-five-degree angle, but the trailer was relatively level. It didn't occur to me initially, but when I reversed back down to hitch up the trailer, neither the twain would meet, let alone combine as one.

No matter how hard I tried, the tow ball just wouldn't fit together with the coupling bit. It occurred to me that no matter how hard I tried to join the two, the angle of the Ford was just not right. I tried to drag the trailer slightly up the slope, and at the same time to try to wedge a piece of timber behind the trailer's wheels. After almost twenty minutes and trying the utmost to give myself a hernia, the rain had begun to fall, I was about to give up when, as if by a bolt from the blue, both pieces came together.

I pulled up the small handle above the coupling bit and managed to secure the trailer to the Ford. Chains attached, and the plug connected, there was only one thing left to do, and that was attempt to drive up the drive and onto the road. All was going well until I suddenly realised that I hadn't retracted the coupling that was covering the tow ball. Does that really matter, I hear you ask?

Of course, if I can cast my mind back a couple of years back, we were staying at the outback Queensland town of St. George in our caravan. There was the instance of a caravanner doing the same thing. One morning this elderly couple was departing the Pelican Rest Caravan Park. He, and it's usually he, forgot to lower his coupling handle onto the tow ball. How do I know what the result of this oversight was? As he and his wife were leaving, a small speed hump needed to be crossed on the way out of the park. Without warning, a loud metallic sound came from over in his direction. Not being one to have a peek at someone's misfortune; if you believe that, you'll believe anything.

Even from my vantage point fifty metres away and behind the nearest bush, I could see what had happened. His tow frame that attaches the car to the van was resting forlornly on the concrete, with the chains still attached. It is especially important to release the handle properly onto the tow ball coupling. When I departed my son's driveway with my trailer, as soon as I hit the road after crossing the gutter, bang, that strange, yet familiar, sound saying, 'something's not connected you, dickhead.'

Foot on the brake pedal, hand brake on, and a quick jump out of the Ford. That's not as easy as it sounds. Although the driveway was a staggering forty-five degrees, the road, on the other hand, was still close to a thirty-degree angle. The need to open the driver's side door was just as difficult as down the bottom of my son's driveway. No matter how old we are, and I must admit the years were catching up with me, I still struggled to prise open the door. I knew immediately what had happened. A quick look around to see if anyone else was witnessing my embarrassment, and thankfully, no one was there to see my trailer still attached to the safety chains, but the frame was left sitting on the road. With a power not known to man, I quickly pulled the trailer frame back onto the tow ball, lifted the handle up and reattached all the bits-and-pieces.

After all that excitement, and I say that with my tongue firmly planted in my cheek, it was time to head back down the hill and tackle the jungle. Having first removed the row of carefully manicured rosemary plants, the next area was a vast swathe of both ivy, roses and the ever-present blackberry plants that had somehow crept into the garden. I had decided that a plan was required. In the past, the method of extraction was to pull everything out, leave it in a pile and wait until the pile was so overwhelming it could wait for another day to be attended to.

Knowing full well what was in store, I took the opportunity to dig, cut, pile, place into my broken wheelbarrow and then wheel the bundle back up the garden path and toss the whole bloody lot into the trailer. They' say, 'oh, it does feel like an Indian summer this autumn.' Not having ever experienced an 'Indian summer' and possibly never will, I can only presume it's bloody hot when it shouldn't be so. Late March in 2021 in Bright the weather was really far too hot for a person of a certain age to be toiling away, removing his jungle when the temperature was reaching the high twenties. Cool nights are a blessing in Bright at this time of year, but, really, digging out a jungle shouldn't be on the agenda.

It wasn't long before perspiration was running off my forehead, down my nose and off my chin. "Am I really doing this?" I muttered to myself. There was no one to witness my endeavours let alone the results that were beginning to be obvious. 'Others' were happily cocooned inside with the air conditioner on.

The ultimate aim and rewards were going to purchase and lay a vast quantity of instant turf over the entire area. That was a long way off, so it was back to the spade, crowbar and rake. After what seemed to be hours of toil, but in reality, just over an hour and a half, progress was being made.

Lost garden gnomes were recovered as were several lonely golf balls. They, of course, were the relics left over from our two sons and their attempts to hit golf balls around the back garden. Now that I think of it, there were times when the challenge to each other was to see whether they could hit a golf ball with a seven iron over the house and onto Delany Avenue. Today that would have been a dangerous and stupid thing to try. With the constant stream of traffic, something or someone could have been hit by a wayward golf ball, but back twenty-five years or so, it wouldn't have been an issue.

Along with the lost golf balls, garden gnomes, and an assortment of long-forgotten metal garden objects, the ground was beginning to be cleared. Progress was being made, or so it seemed. No matter how much ivy was dug up, torn out and raked, there always was more. Do I continue to attempt to extract the ivy entirely? Or is close enough, good enough? The latter of course. Having laid the 'Sir Walter' instant turf a few years ago in the other half of the lawn area, I knew that the stuff was incredibly tough and resilient. So much so, that when established, it strangled everything in reach, weeds, other types of grass and even small stones. Definitely my type of grass.

Although I really did attempt to remove what was left, whatever was hiding under the surface, could really just stay there and let nature take its rightful course. All around the garden were rocks. Dozens of the things. When we were establishing our back garden, my mission in life was to source as many rocks as possible. Mainly to be used as edges for our numerous gardens that were popping up in both front and rear gardens. It always amused me, but when I went out looking to discover that golden pile of rocks that would make my trip a lot quicker, those bloody rocks disappeared. Was someone else collecting them for the same purpose, who knows?

Rocks can be elusive to find, but I do recall one of my more interesting times. That was on Mystic Drive, just past the last of the houses in the area. There I was, quietly minding my own business, walking up and down the dirt road, not a soul in sight. Suddenly, I stopped, and then the bush exploded twenty metres in front of me. A massive stag, antlers, and all, tore through the bush, took one look at this strange shape collecting rocks, and galloped, do stags gallop? Who knows? But it sounded like a herd of racehorses leaving the starting gates. Within seconds, it was across the other side of the road, followed by a pall of dust. Disappearing in moments, what was I to do?

Back into my small truck, turned around and headed for home. That certainly was enough excitement for one quiet Sunday afternoon. Anyhow, back to the garden. All those hundreds of rocks, large and small, now were emerging from their resting places. I don't know if they get larger over time, or with the aging process, they all seem to be larger and heavier. As a matter of interest, a couple of the larger ones that needed to be moved from the front nature strip when our wonderful Alpine Shire came up with the great idea; let's construct the new tarred footpath or, should I say, bike racetrack at the front of the Badrocks front fence. Anyway, back to those bloody rocks. Not your normal sedimentary types, small, flat, and easy to lift, no, these were great lumps of quartz. Hard and heavy enough to roll from one location to the other but try heaving them onto the back of a small truck. I really have no recollection of how I managed the feat, but on this occasion, a couple needed to be shifted. I look at these each time I walk or drive past them and think to myself, 'they should be there for eternity, as no one else would be as stupid as me to attempt such a thing.'

It was now getting to the good part of this saga. Most of the jungle had been cleared, and the surface prepared for the laying of the 'Sir Walter' instant turf, or as we really call it, grass. There were only a couple of options locally to purchase the turf. Bunnings, the great Australian home of hardware things and the Bunnings barbeques. Our nearest store was just down the Great Alpine Road at Wangaratta. Eighty kilometres each way. The other nearest store was in Wodonga, closer to one hundred kilometres from Bright.

Already having my trailer full of a couple of cubic metres of garden refuse, there was no other option but to empty the back of our Ford Everest and drive down to 'Wang,' as we locals call it, and see how many slabs of turf I could jam into the back. I did call prior to making the trip just to make sure there was stock on hand. "Yes, sir, you are lucky, we have a delivery come in every Wednesday afternoon around .three thirty pm." So, off I went first thing the next morning. Knowing how popular this grass was, I ensured I arrived just after eight a.m. To my shock, someone had already been and purchased half the pallet load. Thankfully, there was enough left for me to buy what I needed. With my Bunnings trolley loaded, I made my way out and began loading the fifteen slabs into the rear of the Ford. It's funny how when we try to gauge, or in my case, guess, how large the rear area of the Ford was, it was beginning to look a lot smaller with each slab of instant turf being loaded into the back.

The first ten or so went in without a problem. It was the remaining five that were obstinate. With centimetres to spare, the final three were simply tossed into the space below the roof of the Ford. Having made the effort to try and keep the boot area reasonably clean since we purchased the vehicle, all that hard work went out the window, so to speak. At least the turf seemed to be reasonably clean and dry, just a few smudges on the inside of the roof.

When I returned home, the fun part could begin. Wheelbarrow a few at a time, place carefully into position, stand back, and enjoy the moment. It didn't take long at all before the area I had prepared was covered, the only thing was, to begin the process of removing the remaining area of the jungle. As the next delivery of good old 'Sir Walter' wasn't due in for another week, the area around the garden shed and paved patio area was my next target.

More concrete ducks, strange metal rows of ants and long-lost golf and tennis balls wrapped on one side with grey tape emerged from the latest minefield. One thing I hadn't taken into consideration was the landmines, or in this instance, copious amounts of dog poo. In the past, one had to toss the stuff somewhere, never thinking that I would ever see the stuff again. With each step into the ivy and other assorted detritus, I could instantly feel the unmistakable softness associated with discarded dog shit.

That said, my degree of enthusiasm, showed no bounds. Nothing a good, old pair of worn out- track shoes couldn't cope with. Gloves? They were for sooks. As I continued my quest to retake the garden from the 'jungle gods,' a space resembling a few metres square began to appear. More garden waste to the trailer, but, and there is always a but, the novelty was beginning to wane. What's more, there was now no more space in the trailer after the recent clearing.

A couple of days later, it was off to the tip. Or should I say the Porepunkah Recycling Centre. Only open Wednesdays, Fridays, and the weekends. Four hours only, from ten a.m. to two p.m. With the rules and regulations that our government now considers important, there is now no such thing as backing your vehicle to the rim of a gigantic hole and tossing everything in. Now things need to be separated, consigned to the metal, green waste or concrete piles and only then are we permitted to make our way to the large steel containers to dispose of the rest.

Having now a clear and empty trailer, the next thing was to make the trip down to Wang and purchase another load of Sir Walter. I make the necessary call to make sure the turf was there, "Hello, garden department, Joy here, how can I help?" "I'm just making sure you have good old Sir Walter in stock." "I know we're expecting a delivery, so you should be okay to collect it when you arrive." Great, so off I went with hope and expectation, as this time I needed to purchase thirty slabs of the grass.

Not being the best at reversing my trailer, it was fortuitous that there were several drive-through trailer parking spaces free. I made my way into the store and the garden area. "Hello," I said to the helpful lady in red. "Just wondering where your instant turf is. I phoned earlier and was told it was in stock." "Let me check, what was your name?" She spoke to someone in the office, and by the look on her face, I could tell things were not going according to plan. Well, my plan actually.

"I do believe the person you spoke to earlier gave you the wrong information. Our delivery doesn't come in till around three-thirty this afternoon. Can you come back then?" The lovely lady in the red apron. "Yes, no problems, I'll just drive back to Bright, but can you assure me there will be thirty pieces of Sir Walter for me when I return?" "As you have been somewhat inconvenienced, we'll make sure it will be on a pallet, wrapped and waiting for you later in the afternoon."

When I returned, my wife wasn't impressed. I explained the situation, had lunch, messed around in the garden, and then drove the eighty kilometres back down the Great Alpine Road to Wang. To my delight, it was waiting for me on a pallet and wrapped in plastic. I made my way into the Trades Area making sure that there was no need to reverse anywhere in the building. Instantly two others in red aprons took control of the delivery. "Please remain two paces away and we will load your trailer." All was beginning to look satisfactory. The forklift lifted the pallet into position, lined up with the back of the trailer and pushed and pushed the pallet until it was jammed in so tight that pieces of plastic and turf were beginning to be extruded through the steel mesh sides or the frame. Did I care? Of course not. I was simply happy to drive off back to Bright for the second time, a total of three hundred and twenty kilometres for the day.

Back home, there was no way I could possibly reverse my trailer and Ford into our tight driveway. The only way to complete the exercise was to park on our front nature strip and run the gauntlet of our local Alpine Shire parking inspector. 'Stuff it,' I thought, 'I'll just unload my Sir Walter a few strips at a time into my wheelbarrow. A quick wheel around to the back garden, toss the turf into place and repeat the process.' Six trips later the ordeal was over, and the result was instant. Three-quarters of the area was now covered, I didn't calculate the area to be covered well enough. There was always next week.

In the interim, while I waited for next Thursday to come around, there was a patch of bamboo that had been growing at an alarming rate over recent years. Located quite close to the rear of our house, originally the area was a small section of lawn. Not grass but real lawn.

"Why don't you mow over the top of the bamboo, and we'll turn it into a new sitting area to enjoy the rest of our garden," said my wife. I don't know about you, but has anyone had the desire or need to mow over a forest of backyard bamboo? I knew that this would almost be impossible. When you consider that bamboo could grow close to a metre overnight without watching it, our resident patch, four metres by three metres and over four metres in height was going to take a bit more than just 'a mow.'

Bright and early one morning in early autumn, and with a minor dose of enthusiasm, out I went to where the old metal clothesline once stood. Having a faint memory that somewhere in the vicinity was the decommissioned septic tank. In a failed attempt to contain our lovely thicket of decorative bamboo with another ring of rocks, they were the first to be removed. Not ideal, but they had to be tossed away into the nearest garden bed.

The next task was fighting my way into the mass, one bamboo plant at a time. Each needed to be cut off at ground level and thrown in a pile. The smaller ornamental variety wasn't too difficult. My trusty, long-handled cutters were capable of hacking through stems up to a centimetre in thickness. The much larger ones were a completely different matter. "Why don't you use your new chainsaw, Graham?" said my advisor from the open window in the kitchen.

The novelty of cutting each bamboo plant off near the ground was beginning to take its toll. Some of the more mature plants were close to twenty-five millimetres in thickness. A newly purchased pruning saw was far more manageable than me wielding a chainsaw and slashing everything not in sight. I had already managed to sever the extension lead around Christmas time that flicked the electrical safety switch. Although I had removed the lead from the socket around the side of the house, there was no way I was going to tempt fate again. Seeing two neglected leads lying among the bamboo there was no way I was going in to slash and cut with the chainsaw.

It felt a lot like Indiana Jones attacking some unforeseen foe. Not knowing what was behind the next clump of bamboo. A light grey object with a black electricity cord attached was the first to come to light. It was the remains of a water pump used to pump water into the pond to create a fountain of sorts. When it was my wife's 'great' idea many years ago to put in a pond so that our bed and breakfast guests could have somewhere to sit and admire their reflections in, 'we need a fountain,' said my wife. I do realise that in a previous story I have related the saga, but for those who haven't read about it, or those who have simply forgotten, it goes something like this.

n the peak of summer, a couple of decades ago when we were running our bed and breakfast, there was this space that I was now attempting to reclaim. "Don't you think it would be a great idea if we dug a pond for our guests to enjoy on a hot summer's evening?" said my wife. How could I resist such a challenge? I knew the old concrete septic tank was next to our proposed aquatic wonderland.

I did take the precaution of digging the hole a small distance from the tank, but from then on didn't give it a thought. The dimensions of 'our' pond were about a three-and-a-half metre diameter round excavation with the centre approximately 700mm in depth. For some inexplicable reason, I chose one of the hottest days in Bright known to man.

The fact that it was exceedingly obvious that the ground had not been dug over for an awfully long time as before long, bits and pieces had begun to appear with every spade full of earth that was being removed from the pit. Old, and I mean incredibly old, handmade nails, a couple of ancient padlocks, a small ceramic head with Asian features, and numerous bits of broken glass and shards of pottery. Had I come across an ancient site? I really don't think so, maybe the original owners had simply dug a hole and tossed all their rubbish in. The interesting thing was when we purchased the property at the end of 1992, we were told that over the other side of the road was the original Chinese settlement in Bright. Subsequent research has shown that Hung Fee's Hotel, Joss House, and other various buildings were still there when one of our neighbours was a young child. Maybe they were the culprits, crossing the road in the dead of night and tossing their rubbish onto our then, vacant land. Who knows? But it does make a good story.

Anyway, back to the pond. After what seemed to be days of toil, sweat, and swearing, the hole was complete. We cannot call it a pond until there is water in it. The only option in our little bubble in the world was our local hardware store, Crispies. One of the real original hardware stores that are hard to find today in Australia. I can presume that the tyranny of distance ensures Crispies still exists. A place where the staff are only too happy to cut your timber to size, sell you a bolt or two and offer advice when you need it. There was no chance there would be a specific pond liner, so the other option was to purchase a large piece of black plastic. This too was cut to size to suit my pond. Going with safety, I purchased three large pieces to cover the excavation and allow enough plastic to drape over the edges and onto the ground.

Now came the good part. Toss in the plastic and start filling it with water. Once the water had reached the normal ground level, the plastic had begun to settle into the space below. A problem was now arising; the water had begun to drag the plastic down below the ground level and was threatening to overflow back behind the liner itself. The only thing to do was stop filling, go out into the bush, and find another hundred or so rocks. I think you can now appreciate how the Badrocks have accumulated their own quarry load of rocks over the past thirty years.

With the remaining bamboo quivering with anticipation that this day was going to be their last, a couple of clumps were still holding court between the old, corrugated iron fence and a long-forgotten stump that had emerged when the clearing was complete.

Another couple of surprises were a couple of solar lights still in position at the top of the corrugated iron fence, although I suspect that it had been years since they had been exposed to the sun. Right beside those was a metal hanging basket still attached to the original metal bracket. One other water pump mechanism came to the surface as did the remains of an old tap and broken bits of terracotta piping.

The removal was almost complete. Harping back to my wife's comment, 'why don't you just mow it all?' it was all too obvious that now it had to be dug out by hand. My first attempt with a spade could be compared with someone trying to remove a nail from a fence with a spoon. Not impossible, but totally useless.

It was beginning to become apparent that progress was going to be slow and steady. Steady in the way that, after each root clump was extracted and tossed into the wheelbarrow, I needed to have a quiet moment of reflection. 'Was this bloody necessary?' Having moved past the point of no return, there was nothing else to do but continue heaving the crowbar up and down until the next piece had been broken away.

The obvious thing was that although I had begun on the left-hand edge of the area, I knew that at some time I would come across the old septic tank. Hoping like hell that the top of the tank could provide a solid base so that the bamboo wasn't totally embedded into the ground, rather than sitting on top. Although the original ground had been level with the rest of the garden, due to neglect, or the natural build-up of leaf litter and dog poo, the area that I was now attempting to win back was close to forty centimetres in height and completely bound together with a variety of ornamental and wild bamboo roots.

With a bit more effort than the last, I made contact. Steel on concrete has a certain tone, especially as I would find out shortly. The only option at this time in the removal was to toss all the removed topsoil minus the roots off to the left and keep on excavating. 'Clang' the sound immediately shouted, 'stop and proceed with caution.' Slowly the area of concrete was expanding with each spade full. Eager to see how large the top of the tank would be, a little more enthusiasm than was possibly necessary. A hole about the size of a small notebook appeared on the surface. 'Would it hold my weight?' I wondered. Carefully and with a fair degree of trepidation, I continued with my quest to reclaim the area.

The further I went, the larger the area of concrete became apparent. I really had no idea how large the tank was, but time would tell. After another three wheelbarrow loads of removed bamboo, it was time to take stock of the situation. With one more slam of the crowbar, one more hole appeared. This time larger than the first. Curiosity got the better of me. I went down to the rear of our garden and found a long pole that was leaning against the garden shed wall. Taller than me, which wasn't really that hard, but the length of my post was close to 1.8 metres.

As I lowered the post down, it seemed to take ages for the post to reach the bottom of the tank. A strange hollow sound accompanied by sloshing of water in the bottom made me take a cautionary step back off the edge of the concrete roof. To my surprise, the tank was close to the whole length of my measuring pole. I was now in a bit of a predicament. Do I continue while standing on top of the tank between two holes or reassess the situation?

Common sense prevailed. I made my way around to the fence side and began attacking from the rear. It really does sound like an army manoeuvre, but I was at war with my once beloved patch of wild bamboo. And who was winning, I hear you ask?

It wasn't long before another remanent appeared through the surface. From what I can gather, all old septic tanks needed to have an access point to pump out the waste when the tank was full. There it was, standing proud two hundred millimetres above the surface of the concrete, but in my case, I had already broken the small concrete cap, and that was sitting in two pieces at a forty-five-degree angle.

As someone said, and I think it was one of Australia's former prime ministers, Malcolm Fraser, 'life wasn't meant to be easy,' I knew it was time to take a break from bamboo removal, when, as each day progressed, I was having more and more difficulty standing and moving my arms and shoulders. Was it a case of overdoing these activities, or just old age catching up? I would have thought possibly both.

The week had come around and it was time for the last drive down the Great Alpine Road to Wang to secure the last ten slabs of good old Sir Walter turf. I made sure the turf was in stock for the last area 'down the back.' There was no need for the trailer as ten pieces would be adequate.

The stock was on hand, but where was it? It is usually near the exit door in the outdoor garden area. Prime position, ready for the buyer to load onto one of their trolleys, you know the type, ones that can only be moved by going backwards. I really thought supermarket trolleys could be obstinate pig-headed male things, but I was wrong. Bunnings ones are far worse. There is no way one of the larger ones can be propelled forwards. I have tried this manoeuvre several times always with bad results. The trolley pusher and, in my case, the bloody thing has a mind of its own. Not content to suddenly veer off into the nearest shopper but can take the scenic course into the nearest collection of brooms, rakes, power tools and any other thing that takes its fancy.

So, there we were, my trolley and I are off backwards and heading for the outdoor garden area. The pallet of Sir Walter had been moved to another area of the garden department, as apparently someone had neglected to move the said pallet undercover the previous night. You guessed it. It rained and the pallet was now one gigantic mound of wet and soggy turf combined with a sprinkling of Sir Walter poking through. "Could I please purchase ten pieces of Sir Walter turf, thanks?" I asked the lovely lady in the red apron.

"I am sorry to tell you, I think it could be a bit damp, do you require a few plastic bags to put on the base of your boot?" It was a nice gesture, and I was pleased to accept her kind offer. "Do you need a hand to load it onto your trolley, I'll just go and get myself some gloves?" No sooner had she returned and there we were, loading the wettest, slimiest slabs of turf onto my trolley. The best way to describe what was going into the rear of the Ford was as follows. Most of us in these days of recycling and composting have a container somewhere in our kitchen to toss our unwanted vegetable scraps into before placing them into the compost bin. As I am sure we all know, sometimes, with the best of intentions, the tossing out into the compost bin is overlooked. After a week or so when there is a rich and earthy odour coming from somewhere in the kitchen, a lightbulb goes on in our brain, and we think, 'bugger, I meant to empty that last week.' When the container is finally taken outside, and usually at full stretch, the other hand on one's nose, it's then we see that the decomposing has already begun. A slimy, rank, dark grey matter slides from the container and into the compost bin.

That was exactly what I was being confronted with; good old, slimy Sir Walter on that autumn morning. As we both attempted to slide each slab onto the trolley, bits were breaking off and falling to the concrete. Finally, I paid for my green sludge and made my way out to the Ford. The task was almost impossible, as with each attempt to pour it into the back of the Ford, the now completely brown clay-based stuff felt the need to slide back onto the ground. It was at this point in proceedings that I seriously considered leaving the ten slabs of Sir Walter right where they lay. Do I go back in and purchase a large box of lawn seed and continue along those lines? No, as I had already paid for the stuff, there was no way I wasn't taking it home to Bright.

Eventually, the task at hand was completed and both Sir Walter and I made our way back to Bright. The same procedure was completed this time but in reverse. At least this time the clay-backed, green slimy bits simply slid out the rear of the Ford and into my wheelbarrow. It wasn't long before the task was completed. Did I stand back as before and admire all my hard work? Of course not. This time my hands, shirt, shorts, and shoes were covered in wet clay with a few sprigs of Sir Walter stuck all over the place, I simply needed to be clean and dry. There was absolutely no need to water in the turf as there was enough moisture around to almost toss a model boat onto and enjoy a quiet sail.

As I am writing this, there still are hundreds of rocks to be relocated, maybe back into the bush, if I feel that motivated. The remaining stand of bamboo is beginning to sprout, the dog is pooping all over my new patch of Sir Walter and the autumn leaves, as attractive as they are, need to be raked and tossed into the compost bins. The rest of our house needs to be painted on the outside. I did manage through our COVID-19 lockdown to repaint seventy-five percent of the outside, but as we say, 'there is always tomorrow, the next week or even next year.'

The End